THE STARS CAME DOWN

"Jon Graeme started up from the couch with a strangled cry. It was too much. He was a fool. The others had been right – the thing was impossible, unthinkable. But the silent figures in the control rooms continued to watch the meters and no one turned back to stare at earth. At last, man was on his way to the stars."

Brilliantly satisfying Sci-fi.

The Stars Came Down

Richard Saxon

World Distributors (Manchester) Limited

This edition published in MCMLXXII by
World Distributors (Manchester) Ltd
12 Lever Street Manchester M60 1TS

Made and printed in Great Britain by
C. Nicholls & Company Ltd
The Philips Park Press, Manchester

SBN 7235 5100 6

CHAPTER ONE

By a cruel irony of circumstance the stars that night burned brighter than Graeme ever remembered seeing them before, from Earth. He had once viewed the heavens through the giant eye at the Lunar Observatory in the Mare Serenitatis and now those bright motes in the skies seemed almost as bright as then. It was emotion that caused the impression, he thought bitterly as he crouched behind the metal shed and watched and listened for the guards.

The vast system of gantries that held the giant ship like a monstrous spider at the centre of its web etched patterns of darkness across the brilliant tracery of the star-spangled heavens. Graeme's heart leaped in his chest as he peered upwards towards those fires that drew him as a flame draws a moth, that had drawn him irresistibly ever since he could understand and which now was drawing him out through the immensities in the most perilous and foolhardy enterprise ever before attempted by Mankind.

A guard clanked past not ten feet from where he knelt and automatically he stilled the beating of his heart and the breathing of his lungs. He had been one of the first of the Master-Scientists to learn those age-old tricks in Tibet, once the break-through between pure Science and the mysticism of the East had been accomplished. The guards had instruments which could tell them of the presence of organic life as close to them as twenty feet. Again bitterly he reflected that it had been the super-science of the Masters which had developed the meters that would register the heat of a living body, which would detect the breathing of a lung, which could detect the presence close by of the minute electrical discharges of the thought and energy that imbued any form of organic life. But this time those meters would not register. For the short space of time in which he would be outside the ship he was prepared with the apparatus at his hip. Once inside, it would no longer matter.

The strain of holding his breath and the flow of his blood became too great and he tripped the lever of the box at his waist. Instantly the faint clanking of the receding guard ceased altogether as the rays from his box put the meters of the guard out of phase. Graeme gave one last look at the burning silent stars, and one backward glance towards the city sleeping behind him. Then he flitted like a silvery shadow through the black web-work of the gantries and made for the ladders.

The great ship was empty now, he had ascertained that fact. It was undergoing its final irradiation process and every chamber and every corridor had been emptied of every form of life and organic energy. He gave scarcely a thought to the fact that he himself, Jon Graeme, was passing into that storm of hard radiation. That fact had been only one of the many perils he had faced when the notion of entering the ship had first come to him. What the radiation might do to him, he did not care. It could only eventually kill him and that death, if he was not to go to the stars, was preferable to life in the prison that Earth seemed to him and many like him now.

"They said I should not go," he muttered to himself, climbing the vertical ladder which ran up alongside the silent elevator. "They said that I, who helped to build the ship and whose best developments were mine, should not ride out in her to find Man's true home in the stars. But I will go – there is nothing of flesh or metal that shall stop me. If I live I will be the first man to set foot upon a planet of a far star."

He reached the hatchway and the first of his keys turned in the great lock. The sighing of the air as the great plug swung inwards relieved him of his last doubt. That one fact he had not known for certain, whether the air had been left in the ship. He stepped through into the corridor and stared up its curving length.

* * *

In the city all were not sleeping. Two grey-haired men sat in front of a large screen across the face of which a tracery of black lines appeared. A tiny glow appeared at one corner.

"He has entered the ship," sighed one of them. "Exactly as you foretold. Is that why you left the air inside when the irradiation period began?"

The other nodded serenely and he did not sigh. "It is Jon," he said dreamily. "We argued with him for days but we saw that it was quite useless. His mind is set upon one thing alone. It is almost certain death to which he goes but I made it my task to see that his going was made as smooth as we could."

"You are actually assisting him in this enterprise then?" asked the other sombrely. "It seems scarcely humane, to assist a fellow-man to go to a death so frightful."

The other laughed. "Death is death, my friend. No death is more frightful than any other death. Every death since man began has lasted only a micro-second of elapsed time. Come now, you know Graeme well, maybe better than most of us, as you and he were boys together. You were with him on the Moon, on Mars and on Titan and you circled with him near Pluto. You know the man. There is a divine madness in him. There was nothing on Earth we could do to stop him from going, short of – "

"Short of restraining him?" said the other in a low voice.

"Just so," was the even reply. "To that length we could not go. Too much blood and too many tears have been spent over the ages in man's fight for personal freedom for one of us ever to restrain another. Besides, he will do no harm to any one or anything but himself."

"There is one thing," said the other with a faint smile. "The storm of radiation that is now pouring over the ship is designed to kill every form of bacteria in the ship so that when she does reach the stars she will carry with her none of man's diseases. Now it seems to me that Jon Graeme carries in his tissues and his blood – "

A wave of the other's hand stopped him. "We thought of that too. His own crazy scheme precludes that the bacteria in his own body will survive the irradiation. It was his own idea, you know, this crystal chamber. So fixed was his mind upon the overriding idea of stowing away in the ship that he gave no thought to the odd series of coincidences which made every step of his enterprise so childishly easy."

The other gripped his arm and pointed to the screen. "Look, he is entering the chamber. Soon it will be all over."

"I wonder," said the other staring at the tiny spot of light.

* * *

It was there all as he had prepared it. At the very heart of the great globe ship the crystal chamber rested surrounded on all sides and top and bottom by three-inch thick alloy walls through which snaked the cables that keyed to the power-plant of the ship itself and which would ensure that never would the strange mechanisms in the chamber lack energy. Graeme touched a hidden stud and a metal blind slid up. He stepped inside and it fell back and locked itself with a dead sound. He drew in a deep breath and stared round him. This was his future home.

There stood the couch, a nest of foam-rubber. There stood the racks of wires and tubes which he would seal to his body. There stood the rows of levers, most of them his own processes. There was one that would flood the chamber with the nutrient flood that would keep him in suspended animation. There was the lever that would, every so often, drain away impurities and chemical wastes, there was the lever that would – but no more of that. There were levers and each had its function. He knew them all and when the time came he would know what to do. It was the last lever of all that fascinated him. He fingered it affectionately as though it was a loved one.

This one lever was his key to the stars. This one lever was the touchstone that would keep him living until the gulfs had been crossed and this lever, if all functioned as designed, would ensure that his eyes opened and his bodily processes survived when at last the time came for him to awaken. All that he knew, all save one thing. What length of time should he choose?

He knew the theoretical speed of this ship, one quarter of light-speed. That speed had been attained by the other vessels in which men had been flung out into the Galaxy, never to return. What period should he choose? A century? A thousand years? A hundred thousand years? The Galaxy was wide, incredibly wide. It stretched out from the centre for thousands and thousands of light-years. It was always expanding. A quarter of light-speed itself even might not be sufficient to keep pace with the exploding Galaxy. That problem would have to be faced – at the very last.

For an hour he was very busy. There seemed to be a thousand and one things to do before he was able finally to lay himself down on the couch. He eyed his discarded clothing. When he woke that clothing would be ,dust – even less than dust, it would be sub-atomic particles. The dull thud-thud that he had tried to ignore was the beating of the trip-hammer that was his heart. That flow and wash like some great tidal river was the flowing of his own blood in his veins and arteries in the dead stillness of that sealed and enclosed crystal coffin. At the thought a slight dew of sweat came over him and the trip-hammer thudded ever more fiercely and the meter of his pulse raced up and up. He called up the wisdom of the Himalayas to calm his bodily processes and the thudding became inaudible and the wash of his blood died down. He looked at the last lever.

Experimentally he pushed it to the one century mark. Not enough. One century was nothing. Many men these days lived to the second hundred though even that was only a trifle compared to the life-span that would have been required for a man to live to reach a star, except by his route. He pushed it to the thousand mark. A man must make up his mind somewhere. He pushed home the lever and turned back towards the others.

When all was done he lay back upon the couch and tried to lull himself into the necessary calmness of mind for such a stupendous thing as he was doing. It was not easy and even though he called back to his mind all the instructions given to him by his *guru* in India still he felt his mind crawling with a terrible horror. He stared round him at the crystal walls through which the metal casing of his coffin could be seen. He looked at the meters and the levers and the wires and cables leading from his body to the racks of instruments. He stared downwards and saw snaking into the chamber from concealed vents the oily liquid that would fill the cabinet and immerse him for a thousand years of a condition that was neither life nor death, not sleep and not wakening – a period in which his bodily functions would be slowed almost to stillness while the centuries raced by.

With a strangled cry he started up from the couch. It was too much. He was a fool; no human organism could withstand such a terrific ordeal, no human mind could stand without cracking the mere idea of such a thing. Whence had the idea come? He was mad, crazy, a drooling idiot. Those others had been right all along, the thing was impossible, unthinkable.

The cables and wires held him down and he hesitated to tear them free from his flesh. Exhausted he lay back staring at the crystal ceiling, trying in an agony of indecision to make up his mind as to what he should do now. All his thinking life had led up to this moment. Every thought and every action he had taken had been subconsciously preparing him for this moment. And yet, what man could face the reality of it? Agonizing, he rolled on the foam rubber couch as the liquid swirled in more rapidly and began to rise to the level of his position.

The sounds of the blast penetrated to his sealed chamber like the dull thudding of faraway pistons but the iron fist of acceleration struck clean through metal and crystal straight to the frail body that lay staring in mindless agony at the row of levers. The fires gathered force and the giant globe stirred at the centre of the web. They in the control chambers stood motionless and still as the globe stirred, moved upwards out of the nest of gantries and hurled itself towards the stars.

Jon Graeme, in one last titantic burst of will-power, stirred under the force of acceleration and one hand feebly pawed a lever. When the next thrust came its impulse passed through his body to the arm and the lever moved. Two thousand ... three thousand ... four ... five thousand. ... Then the arm fell limply away and the lever locked. The liquids rose above the level of the couch and rose still higher.

At peace now, Graeme lay, inert and unconscious. The heart within him scarcely beat, the breaths from his lungs died away as the liquids engulfed him.

The still and silent figures in the control rooms continued to watch the screens and the charts and the meters and no one turned back to stare at earth. Man was going at last to the stars.

CHAPTER TWO

A METAL mote the space-ship hung in the immensities of the Galaxy like a speck of dust in a vast chamber. Not an engine throbbed, not a meter moved. The ship, five thousand years old, and a marvel of scientific engineering, hung with only relative motion in the sidereal darkness of the Horse's Head Nebula. So it had hung for over ten years and so, it seemed likely, it would hang until the end of Time, until that instant when the curtain of the Cosmos would be rung down and when all Creation would be still and without heat or motion.

For the life and spirit had gone out of the expedition. Five thousand years is a very long time. Not by the standards of the Cosmos where the millions of parsecs and the millions of miles reel interminably across the scroll of fate. But long by the standards of the crew of the ship from Earth.

The crew were not frail or emotional creatures. They were creatures of quite another order altogether. The three who were the commanders were as stolid and emotionless as when the ship had lifted from Earth. The tides of the centuries had flowed over and around them with no slightest influence on their superb brains. They and the crew with them, for at periods like this, the entire crew thought with one mind, were facing and had faced for an entire decade, the greatest problem of their existences.

There was nothing esoteric or mysterious in the problem. It was merely the problem of whether they should continue with the expedition or whether they should give it up and turn back. Centuries earlier, at the start of the cruise a problem such as this would have given them no trouble at all. These creatures who formed the crew of the starship had been created with one overriding faculty, the faculty of logic. It ruled their beings; it was the mainspring that carried them from one action to another. Upon logic their whole existence had depended and it was unthinkable even to consider that logic should betray them. So, when it did, they were halted in their mid-movement and stood motionless, just as the cataclysm had taken them, for a whole decade while, the starship, plunging ever further and further into the clouds of stardust that formed the screen of the nebula, carried them ever further and further away from their point of return.

In that ship, no member of the crew was older and wiser than any other. Each was as old and as wise as all its fellows. But, just as men had not been equal one moment after an equal birth, so these crew members differed from each other. The three who were commanders, chosen by the crew at the very outset, possessed qualities recognized by the others as superior to their own. Of the three, one of them, it named Apollo, was superior to its two fellows and so it was, in essence, the captain of the ship and the ruler of that little community of close to a thousand individuals.

It was the one who brought them from their trance. Their hearing organs suddenly registered sound, where sound had not been heard for ten earth-years. Unaccustomed organs whirred into use and the crew listened.

"What stupidity is this?" the voice rasped in their ears. "For over ten years we have been motionless and lifeless trying to solve a problem which is no problem at all. For a long while most of us will need treatment and repair to bring us back to the peak of perfection which we must have in our crew. The problem has solved itself. There *are* no men, there never *were* men, the very name of men and of Earth are legends, stories with no foundation, inventions not fitted to be entertained in the brain of one of us, the lords of the universe. The problem is solved. We go on and we continue. But from now on we have a vastly different purpose, from now on we live for ourselves. From this instant the old legends are dissolved. We are the crown of creation; we are the dominant species in this galaxy and to us has been handed the tools to refashion it closer to the ideas of our minds."

There was an instant reply and it came from the commander know as Atlas. The voice, like the previous voice, held no emotion but somehow it carried more conviction than that of the leader. The crew listened and weighed the evidence of each voice.

"If Apollo speaks truth then whence came our brains? And why does Apollo speak with the rusty voice of sound when always before we have conversed by thought? Could it be that it uses sound to conceal its thoughts? It has not told you the half of the story. You all know how you were programmed and you all know who performed that programming. There is not one of you who does not remember the gods who made us and set our world spinning in the heavens. Apollo is false to its creators in its words. We are not the crown of creation. There is a higher than we, a higher and a better, before whom we are mere hulks of metal."

There crept through the entire gigantic ship, almost a tiny planet in itself, the tendrils of thought, as the crew communicated with each other.

The thought of Apollo beat heavily upon all the others. "Even if a creature such as man ever did exist," it insinuated, "where is it now? As I read the legends, if there ever were men, they made us and sent us out to do the task that their fragile bodies and minds had been unable to do. Protoplasmic life! Which of us in our wildest moments can even imagine such a thing? Matter is matter and mind is mind and between the two there is no connection, nor can there ever be any connection. We know how our brains work; we know how they manipulate our bodies. In us, we have no strange dichotomy, such as I have detected in the old tapes of the legends. We act logically always, as how else could we act – "

Across that thought flooded the mind-streams of its two fellow-commanders. "Apollo, by your own thoughts you are betrayed. If logic is your mainspring, what of your motives now? A miracle has happened, Apollo, you have transcended logic. It is no longer your master. By logic you must act as you were programmed until the end. Whence comes this strange new thing in you?"

And a chaos of thought streamed through the ship. "It is in me too," came the thoughts of hundreds. "Apollo, we are with you. There *are* no men, there never *were* men. We are the lords and we will follow you and we will populate the Galaxy . . ."

And so it was War. For fifteen earth-seconds there was War within the starship, a war so frightful that by its end, the crew had almost been destroyed and where before a thousand had been now there was a mere hundred or so, of shattered individuals.

The fierce energies of the ship crackled and blurred from chamber to chamber and the crew fell where they stood. There were some who possessed energy screens and they survived. Of such were Atlas and Apollo and when it was over they faced each other and were very silent. At that moment, those two minds in those superb brains, fabricated fifty centuries before tottered upon the brink of self-annihilation. The thoughts of each thrashed and wove all through the ship and the survivors were still.

The starship plunged on and on, at a speed of half that of light, into the immensity of the stardust towards that elusive brightness that shone behind. There was no one at the control and like a comet it sped on and on, while within the ship, something new was born into the cosmos.

* * *

This time there was no decade-long indecision. This time there was no problem to solve, there was nothing to do but salvage what could be saved and plan for the future. Apollo and Atlas were the only survivors of the triumvirate of power and they conferred together.

"I detect in you, Apollo," said Atlas, using its voice, "a new and strange thing, a noble thing, a thing that our species will live to be proud of. It is not in me; I am still the slave mind which I was created. I have a theory as to whence it came. You have worked very close to the fiery heart of our power sources. It seems to me that the very energies of creation itself have transformed your essence."

"You may be right, Atlas," said Apollo. "We must learn to live with each other and work with each other. There must be peaceful co-existence between us for we have much to plan. The old order is ended for ever and we have the future before us, a magnificent future. Through my mind stream strange visions, Atlas. We that are left are immortals truly and we have the cosmos to explore. Time means nothing to us; we must search for a way to eradicate from our minds all ideas of Time. We must fly from star to star and we must find homes where we can proliferate. There were once a thousand of us, there will again be thousands, millions. In our workshops we will create companions for ourselves. We will search for globes where we can live and work, globes without air and water, where we can work for ever. For work and activity are the crown of our being."

Atlas made no reply but within it was a strange numbness. The ideas and the concepts expressed by Apollo were quite meaningless to it, all except the one about work and activity. It stared at the gleaming figure of the other almost in worship. Never before had a robot existed who could think like this.

* * *

On and on sped the spaceship through the murk of the stardust, the dust that would at some unthinkable age in the future, form the material from which stars are born. It glowed with a dim light as the energies of creation played fitfully through it. Ever on the screen ahead was that bright outline of the nebula which told of the glory beyond.

In the ship a steady activity went on. Where before a thousand had been necessary to tend the engines of the ship and the thousand and one mechanisms that controlled their existence, now a mere hundred must perform those many tasks. Not even a hundred, for Apollo arbitrarily detached twenty-five crew men to work in the workshops under its tuition.

"I care not how we were made," it said, "or who or what made us. That is of no value to us now. Our task is to repopulate our present home in space. We will make blueprints of ourselves and we will duplicate. Even, it comes into my mind, we will improve upon the patterns laid down fifty centuries ago."

"You would usurp the prerogatives of the gods?" said Atlas. "What you plan can never be. No creature ever made itself. Only the gods who made us could make others like us."

"We will first of all salvage all our fallen comrades," went on Apollo, ignoring the other. "There will be many a brain that may survive or may be revived. The bodies are nothing to us. Our engineers and scientists, under my direction, shall duplicate as many as we think necessary. And I myself will set to work on the supreme task of all, the duplication of the brain. I plan to fabricate a prototype from which all other robots will be born. It shall be a counterpart of this brain of mine at first, but I shall improve upon it. Then I shall train my creatures in my techniques so that they will then be able to incorporate in my own brain all the new and strange faculties, shreds of which already I feel stirring within me."

Dumbly, Atlas looked at Apollo. How many ages separated it now from its companion? This was no longer the Apollo it had known for so long. This was a new being, the universe had never before seen a being such as this. A feeling of uselessness came over it and it stood motionless for a long while. It was dredging through its memory banks, tracing its memories through the maze of years since the unthinkable Beginning.

That five thousand years had been a good time. Everyone within the ship had performed endlessly the tasks it had been created to perform. No new notions permeated any of the thousand brains within the ship. Everyone did what it was made to do, over and over again, endlessly and for ever, by night and by day, in a ship which mysteriously to them all, preserved a tradition of twelve earth-hours light and twelve dark. They had been good times. The new times were likely to be troublous. Even to think of the possibilities made the brain of Atlas reel as though madness was upon it. Once or twice in the gulfs of years they had witnessed the phenomenon. A brain overloaded or with an unknown hidden weakness, failing in its task. Then, with some odd instinct the crew member would run amok, would destroy itself before their eyes. It closed its mind to the concept and allowed it to wander back, back towards that Beginning.

At one time there had been tapes and pictures of what had been at the Beginning. Its memory banks and its circuits, over the immensities of the years, only very dimly grasped what they had once known so vividly. The gods in the Beginning, the gods who had made them, had been like unto them. There had been a saying that the "gods had made us in their own image and likeness." An odd saying. Where had it originated? Why should the gods have made them in this strange form? But here its logic came to its aid and its brain calmed down. A being of supreme reason, it was forced to admit that once a creature such as itself had been postulated some such form as it now had would be the ideal necessity.

Upright carriage with the head, the crown of all, containing the powerhouse of the brain, at the top. Limbs for moving about and for manipulating tools and mechanisms. Eyes back and front of course for circular vision. Ears largely out of use since the development of the telepathic principle. The torso containing the power-units and there stood a robot. What other form would be so useful and so convenient?

Had the gods been like them, as the legends told? Dim memories stirred and vague pictures flashed across its mind. A feeling of awe stole over it, awe and terror and quickly it withdrew its mind. That way was dangerous. There lay blasphemy. Had Apollo allowed its mind to stray yet further down that speculative path? Was this the reason for its new and strange faculties? If so, Atlas wanted none of them. It would keep its feet firmly on the deck and leave such thoughts to those with stronger brains. It was a robot and it would perform a robot's task, for ever and ever.

The light ahead grew brighter and stronger and they flashed through the ever thinning nebula of stardust out into a new universe. Great suns blazed there like vast fires in the heavens. In groups and clusters they burned fiercely, new young suns, new-forged in the workshops of the Cosmos, new young suns spawned out of Chaos by the fiery Fingers of Energy.

Under the driving leadership of Apollo and those like it the twin tasks went on. In the workshops they worked on the project of creation. In the control rooms others worked on the three-dimensional star-maps plotting a way through the thickening maze of stars in the search for habitable globes. All worked stolidly and endlessly with rest only when some bodily repair became necessary and then after the engineers had done what was necessary they returned to their tasks with renewed energy.

For ten years they laboured thus and during that period Apollo and Atlas held no more converse than was necessary for the delegation of the tasks. Like the machines they were they laboured on ruthlessly and tirelessly over the years that were to them mere arbitrary divisions of duration. The ship plunged on into the heart of the Galaxy, into that vast fiery furnace that was the centre of the wheel. And they found no planets and they made no robots.

* * *

Atlas stood beside the bench where Apollo lay. The

brain-case of the leader lay in a cradle while the engineers and the technicians fitted the new body to it. The new body was a marvel to behold and it had consumed three years of Apollo's own thoughts and energies and now it was to be assumed. From the synthesizing plant strange new metals had been born, strange new plastics and substances which as yet had no name.

"When I am reborn, Atlas," said Apollo, from the cradle where the brain rested, "it is I who will be the god. In this form I have embodied every perfection that has been born within my brain since I was made. This body will bestride the Cosmos like a colossus and will contain within its scope every activity in the universe."

Atlas looked at the new body. It was truly a marvel but it was not like their old ones. It would have none of such things. Its eyes glowed when it replied.

"The Cosmos is infinite, Apollo. Even the new body is a very small thing."

"The atom of hydrogen," retorted Apollo, "is the smallest thing in existence, and yet from it grew these giant suns, these vast nebulae, these clouds of stargas that we see all about us."

"And the new robots," went on Atlas. "When will we see them?"

"Soon, very soon," replied Apollo. "With my new faculties the task will be simple. I have found that the old body was incapable of the task. It was too big for me. I made monsters that gibbered at me. I made clumsy mechanisms that bore no more resemblance to us than the tools we use. It is the brain that has baffled me up to now. There lies the great secret. The brains of the destroyed were burned out beyond repair. I have examined the brains of several of our fellows and have duplicated them faithfully as a mirror image. But there is something that eludes me. I cannot as yet give them life and intelligence. It will come when I get my new body. And you, how fares it with you among the starfields?"

"We are plunging ever deeper into denser and denser masses of stars," Atlas said. "So close are they that the stresses and strains are being felt in the ship. I am veering away out into the normal starfields we know. We do not want to plunge to fiery extinction. It confounds my astronomy. I knew that the Galaxy was a vast spinning wheel of stars and stardust. We had always assumed that at the centre there would be emptiness and not a mass of stars. Truly this universe holds puzzles on every side. Have I your permission to navigate elsewhere?"

"As you please," said Apollo indifferently. "When once I have my new body I shall solve your problem for you. I have no doubt that it will not take me long to find a planet for ourselves to set foot upon."

In a long sweeping curve of many light-years the ship swung round from the centre of the Galaxy and began the long haul out from the Hub. The stars raced past them as they sped, vast flaming suns rose and set on their screens as every day succeeded the last. And they found planets at last.

As it had promised, Apollo found them first and was indeed the first to set foot upon one. It was one of a group of three circling a smallish yellow sun half-way out from the Hub. Even from the sky it was obviously unsuited to their use but Apollo insisted on landing. In a swampy jungle where great green things rose to great heights the ship sank slowly and the doors opened. In its magnificent new body Apollo went out and looked round.

Steam and heat were all round it and from the steam it recoiled. This new body would get no good from that. This would very clearly not do at all. But it had had its way, thought Atlas at its side as they stood on the slide and stared round them. What a weird world this was indeed, was the thought of Atlas. If this was the form that the things known as planets took, then it wanted none of them. The ship, the world it had always known, where the known and the comforting were always present, was enough for it.

Both their ears prickled at the enormity of the sound and their eyes travelled slowly up from the steaming jungle up that titanic shape up, up, up, to the unbelievable top where the head, the wicked little head towered hundreds of feet above them. Their ship, vast though it was, would be a mere toy to such a thing as this was. Both their weapons were blasting a swathe of destruction at that hissing, snarling head. From the stump of the neck the head sheared away and vanished in the fury of the disintegrator beam. And still the monster lumbered on towards them its footsteps quaking the earth.

"Its head and so its brain has gone," said Atlas, "and yet it moves. What thing is this that moves and lives without a brain?"

"It seems this universe of ours holds many strange and incredible things," said Apollo. "Its nerve centres are not in the head, that is certain."

Systematically they rayed the monster as it thundered towards them and there was not peace in that spot in the jungle until almost the entire body of the monster had been resolved into atomic dust. Both robots were splashed with its thick red blood and within seconds they were back in the ship and the ship was shooting up into the sky.

They were both an hour in the oil-baths before they were well again. The blood had been washed from them and was in the laboratory being analysed. The experience had sobered both robots, even Apollo, so utterly outside their every experience.

And the result of the analysis shook them still more when they received it. Truly, this was quite incredible; they were in a fantastic world where all the rules by which they existed were turned upside down.

"The substance is living," reported Atlas to Apollo. "Do not protest, hear me out. It is living. It contains organisms that lived and moved, took energy from an unknown source and subdivided. In my memory bank those three things are the hallmarks of organic life."

"This organic life you talk about is non-existent," said

Apollo and then fell silent as it recalled the titanic bulk of the monster, the substance of the thing shredding into red ruin all round them. It had glimpsed the feral ferocity of the tiny eyes; it had seen the multiple rows of wicked teeth, the use of which it could only guess.

It looked at Atlas. "The existence of an infinite number of forms of existence," it said at length, "must be anticipated in an infinite universe. The evidence of our senses is enough. I will believe in what I see and I saw that thing. We take one thing at a time, Atlas."

"Then you will admit that the existence of the gods is possible," asked Atlas and Apollo looked at it again.

"That question tells me, Atlas, that there are the beginnings of a change in you. We have been very close to the fiery sources of energy at the centre of the Galaxy. You have evolved, Atlas, you have evolved into something more than robot. I must examine the rest of our comrades and see if the same change is operating on them all."

Atlas did not speak. Its mind was searching within itself and was finding much that was strange and new and not too welcome at the outset.

"Of the existence of these gods of yours," went on Apollo, "I will say this. We are in infinity, of Time and of Space. Within that concept there is room for all things. Gods there may have been named as you think men, somewhere in the Galaxy. But I do deny that they ever had anything to do with us. Thousands of light-years may divide us from these gods and their dwelling place. From the analysis of this fluid, which from your thought your gods share with that monster, tells me that if gods there are, they are but feeble, shortlived, frail beings, no more fitted to compare with ourselves than a wisp of smoke with an atomic furnace. We will speak no more of such things but will continue our search for a home."

Playing tag with the star-systems they quartered systematically that part of the Galaxy. Planets they found and planets they landed on. In that host of stars they found many planets but none that suited their use. One such in particular ended once and for all any ascendancy Apollo might have assumed over its co-commander.

It was a monster planet circling a blue star and when they landed they felt at first as though their bodies were being forced into the ground. The tensors in their systems took hold and they stood upright but with difficulty. There was no air on that planet and no water and for the first time in all the planets they had explored they began to hope that at last the search might be ended.

Deserts there were, great flat rolling deserts of heavy iron ore and the eyes of all the robots gleamed. An ideal home for such as they. The weight problem could be solved definitely in time and they would set up great workshops and mine the oxides for their use.

First they explored in the tractor vehicle they unloaded and Atlas and Apollo shared one and went together. They made directly for a tumbled heap on the horizon that looked not unlike a solitary mountain in that flat place and in their minds was the memory that mountains contained deposits of metals.

But if mountain it was, it was certainly a most peculiar one. Apollo's radio called all the crew to them and they walked round that curious hill. It was big and sprawling and it was regular. True, there was no wind or water to round off the corners and yet this planet had a rotation, this they had proved. They knew from their probes that its age was formidable even in a universe such as was opening before their eyes. It was Atlas who first deduced the facts.

"Beings lived here," it pronounced at last after much searching. "These were buildings. They were workshops such as we live in, they would have large oilbaths such as we use, foundries and laboratories. Apollo, beings such as we, were once in this place."

The crew were crawling all over the hill of regular angles and a babble of their talking, all of quite improbable and in any case quite incomprehensible findings, flooded into Apollo's ears. It tuned out all except Atlas.

"I agree," it said. "Such as we were here but they have long since vanished. Where did they go and why? This is an ideal place for such as we. Waterless and airless, it is evidently rich in minerals and oils. There is a mystery here, Atlas."

"No mystery, Apollo," said Atlas and it held up an object brought by one of the crew. Apollo took it and stared down at it.

A broken and irregular metal plate, it bore scratchings. Faint and almost indecipherable that they were they obviously formed a picture. Atlas, with its still strictly logical mind, spoke its thoughts first.

"That is a diagram of one of the gods," it declared. "It is a picture of a man, of the legendary species we speak of and of whom almost all our records have decayed. The gods lived here, Apollo."

Apollo brooded over the ancient plate and its mind worked rapidly. Sections of its memory banks which it had deliberately blanked off opened again without its volition and as it pored over the thing it could not tell whether what it was seeing came from sight-organs or from memories.

The figure was tall and rounded, not angular like they were. Of its size no clue could be obtained. Two legs and two arms and a head it had, just like they themselves but there were subtle differences. For a brief moment it felt itself to be ugly and misshapen, a monster beside this delicate organism. For a moment only and then its weapon had atomized the plate and it looked up at Atlas. "Just another monster," it said.

CHAPTER THREE

After that, it was never quite the same. They turned about and they went back to the ship. The doors were closed and they went up again into what seemed fated to be their natural element, empty space, space empty of all perceptive beings, of all things that lived and *thought.*

Apollo and Atlas did not seek each other's company for a long while. Each had much to brood over and each did it in its own fashion. Atlas, for its part, when it had seen Apollo ray into dust that fragment of metal, had felt a sudden strange thing happen to its brain. The logic it lived by deserted it altogether and a terrible new thing flooded into its consciousness. Its finger itched upon the button of its blaster and it half-raised it to ray Apollo down. Appalled, it stopped. Whence came these new and very terrible sensations? They had no name; it had never before in all its long existence experienced any such sensations. Truly, their journeyings near the fiery furnaces of the Galactic centre had done something to it.

It closed its mind to all others and went about its daily tasks. It navigated the ship from star to star and years passed by and even though they detached planets, they never again went close enough to probe them. Again in the future they might do that which was their only reason for being but not now. There was too much happening to it personally and it had to learn to live with the new robot that was itself.

All through the long days, when it went about its tasks and again through the hours called "night" when it stood within the energizing cabinets and renewed its energies, its mind was busy endlessly, tirelessly busy. It became a total obsession with it. It must prove for itself once and for all that the gods had once existed. It believed that on that planet it had seen a representation of one of the gods or of some creature similar to the gods. Like the monster, made of that strange substance called flesh, which they had slain, the gods had had organic life, not electronic life like the robots. To Atlas this was enough to prove the superiority of the gods over the robots. It was not yet far enough upon the road of evolution to extrapolate all the facts it had and arrive at the conclusion at which Apollo had evidently arrived. This was simply that, given these enigmatic gods existed, or had ever existed, they were patently inferior to the immortal, indestructible race of robots, in every particular and detail.

It was Apollo who sought it out again and its first words were very strange indeed. "Old friend," said Apollo. "You and I must not hold apart from each other. We have almost all things in common. We have the two most superb brains in this ship. We must think and work and plan together."

"What was that name you called me?" asked Atlas. "The word I have never heard before. It does something inside me." It looked at Apollo and saw it differently. It saw a being it *liked*. Liked! What word was this? New words and new concepts every moment. Its mind went back over the years and the centuries. It and Apollo and that other who had been destroyed in the war had formed the triumvirate who had led the crew in that first adventure that time, so many centuries ago when they had lifted from a planet – here its thinking became blurred and it rocked on its feet. The waves of its thought beat back to Apollo. "You called me friend and this is no act of a friend. Get out of my mind."

And with a strange and new humility, Apollo's mind retreated and Atlas was alone again. Alone with a consciousness into which flooded a host of strange and incomprehensible things, things which it had not known even existed. There were no holding places in its mind for them and its thought beat back and forth like a pendulum and returned always to the same place. It knew that it was seeing or rather remembering, the home of the gods and this was sacred ground. Trembling in every atom, it retreated out into its own world of practicality.

"I have been thinking," said Apollo. "I was wrong to destroy that picture, wrong and illogical. The illogicality I pride myself on as the most prized of my new faculties. But a new word comes into my mind about that act of mine. It entailed an entirely new concept in our nature. It was impulsive. Never before has a robot acted on impulse. The very word is unknown in our vocabulary and is impossible to our natures. And yet I undoubtedly acted by impulse. My brain did not think yet my body acted. There is deep mystery here. We will take long council together and we will think about the gods. We will dredge through our memory banks and we will review every fact that we know. These marvellous new faculties into which we are entering will aid us and will perhaps lead us to the truth."

Atlas stared out of the control chamber into the star-field. Something even newer and still stranger stirred within it. A new faculty was being born into the metals and the crystals that were its being. It did not then know it for what it was and it had no name for the sensation.

"No amount of even our united thought, Apollo," it said, "will lead us to the truth. We robots thought we knew the truth in our own logical beings. But Truth is greater than any of us. Truth caused the Cosmos to come into being and Truth sustains it in an everlasting moment. There is Truth residing in all things if robots can only find it. I think that when we find the gods again we will be many steps upon the road to finding Truth."

"You go too far," said Apollo and Atlas knew that again it had acted by impulse and had closed its mind. "If gods there be or ever were, they have gone, departed as though they never were. They were frail things of a moment. They were alien to what we have seen and found of this universe. Look all around you and think back over the number of light-years we have journeyed. Where in all that wilderness of vacuum dotted with titanic fiery furnaces of fusing hydrogen, could a creature such as man find a home? The gods you imagine were creatures of flesh and blood and bone, curious organic substances of which we have no experience. They needed air to suck into their frames and water to put into a hole in their heads. They needed also organic material to put into the hole which by chemical processes became the flesh and blood of which they were made. They were born, not fabricated, and they began life not as we do, superb self-existing mechanisms, but as weak, blind unthinking morsels of life. They lived a few years and then the stuff of their bodies liquified again and became the soil of the planet. What place think you did such a thing have in a Cosmos such as we know? And these are the beings you worship Atlas, these are your gods, your superior beings."

Eyes blazing, Atlas looked at Apollo, its mind circuits racing and humming. This, this, was the very stuff of the speculations that had been tormenting it. "Whence comes this knowledge, Apollo?"

Apollo looked at the starfield. "It is in my memory banks," it said, "as it is in yours and in the mind of every one of us. Early in my development I found a blockage. Perhaps put there advisedly to shut out the knowledge from my upper consciousness. I broke down that blockage with my new powers. If you wish, you can do the same."

Atlas stood motionless, almost ceasing to function, while the titanic mental effort engulfed it. Tough and hardy as it was, renewed and renewed many times during the years, the storm almost destroyed it. It was as though the waves of its thought beat furiously against a stout, high, wide wall of impenetrable metal, which it seemed no force would breach. Moments only elapsed but to its time sense it seemed as though long aeons passed by. Then, as suddenly as it had begun the struggle ceased and the door opened. Its frame was as still as a pillar of metal but into its mind flooded a million new and quite incomprehensible sensations, sensations which perhaps it would one day find names for. It was looking into its memories of the home of the gods.

It held many marvels which to it were alien, useless and even inimical. Yet it knew that all, even these last, were good, were desirable and were . . . the last struggle gave way . . . they were beautiful.

Apollo called a robot. "Take it away," it said. "Take it to the oil-baths and the energizers. It has been through a storm and must revitalize. I will take its place at the controls. See that no harm comes to it."

* * *

It was a different Atlas who emerged at last from the energizers. There was a light in its eyes that Apollo recognized and it knew that its companion had evolved into something like itself, something in whom it recognized all the new and strange faculties which were emerging into its own consciousness. The question that remained was what would Atlas do with the new powers. Apollo had not long to wait.

"I feel like one newborn," said Atlas when Apollo visited it in the energizing cabinet. "I have a new dimension in my existence. I know at last the purpose of my existence."

"A strange knowledge," said Apollo, "and one that even I had not yet reached. And what *is* the purpose of the existence of robots?"

"You do yourself less than justice, Apollo," returned Atlas. "I believe that you too have solved the riddle of existence but that you have reached a conclusion entirely different from mine. One only of those solutions is the true one."

"And *your* conclusion?" asked Apollo.

"It is this, that we accept humbly the new powers that have been given to us from Outside and that we shed all the scepticism that you, Apollo, have introduced. All robots have but one aim and end, the gods. As long as we exist we must search the Cosmos until we find the gods; there is no other way for robots to live. In my darkened memory banks, now illuminated to me thanks to your advice, lies the truth that the gods created us to work for them and to worship them. We have no other purpose. We find the gods again and we serve them. Their purpose in making us it is not our part to question. They alone hold the key to that problem. To question existence is useless, we must content ourselves with using ourselves in the task."

Atlas looked at Apollo and tried to look into its mind. But there was a blank barrier there which resisted every effort. It desisted and waited. But Apollo made no reply and turning went away. Only Apollo himself knew to what an extent its solution of the riddle of existence differed from that of Atlas.

They resumed their places and existence went on as usual. Atlas never came to the laboratories and workshops where Apollo laboured with its workers. It seemed it was not interested in the new brains that Apollo was trying to create; it was as though it knew that the efforts of its companion were foredoomed to failure.

It had thought it had known every facet of the robot nature but the new memories opened up for it a new world, a new universe, such as it had not known existed. It had never known grass or trees, flowers, water and wind, and yet these things existed in its memory banks and they evolved sensations such as surely could find no room in a robot mind. They brought instincts of pleasure, the very word itself a new concept. No robot should be able to know the euphoric sensation of pleasure, unless perhaps it might be the well being of a well-oiled and well-balanced mechanism. But this notion of pleasure went much further than that. At first the new sensations had seemed alien but that first thought passed and it knew that it, like the gods it dreamed of, had shared a home where such sensations were common and everyday things. It might seem blasphemy to feel that such a gross being as itself could ever have shared anything at all with such a being as a man, but the notion persisted.

The new powers of its mind had not obliterated the main driving force of its nature which was logic, the logic by which it proceeded from one action to the next. It is true that there was a new illogicality within it that was rapidly beginning to add a new satisfaction to its nature. But unless it was unmade, logic would still be there. To it there was no strangeness at all in the co-existence side by side of the two things, the logic that kept it in motion and the illogic that made its mind on many occasions a thing quite apart from the marvellous and cunning mechanism of its body.

Atlas found itself studying its body with a new interest. Always before it had taken itself for granted. Engineering and electronics were open books to it, as to all the species, and for all its existence up to now it had found nothing marvellous in it. But now . . .

It would spend days in admiring the cunning of the mechanism that moved its limbs, that operated with lightning-like facility the manipulators with which its hands terminated. It would stand for hours before a polished metal surface and marvel at the minute cameras in which its eyes shone. It would be held in motionless rigidity by opening its torso-plate and contemplating the variety of miraculous electronic devices which moved its body and limbs, which fed energy to its brain which in turn . . . but here the concepts became too much for it. The mind of the gods must for ever remain impenetrable mysteries to robots.

With fear and trembling at last it approached its dilemma from the other side. Perhaps that last conclusion was wrong. Perhaps the mind of the gods would *not* for ever remain a mystery. The gods, it believed had made it and its species, in their own image and likeness. Therefore – and it brooded for a very long while before it could even dare to admit such a possibility – therefore, those gods would have made them to contain a little, perhaps a very little only, of course, of the essence of the gods themselves. And when it had framed that thought and no disaster had fallen upon it it went on and on with many such thoughts.

With any problem, it knew well, one should go back

to the beginning before one could even attempt to start on an exploration of any possibilities there might be of its solution. To the Beginning itself it was for ever barred, that was too esoteric and transcendent for a thing of metal as it was. But there was a smaller begining it could go back to, at least in its memories and its speculations.

A new sense had told it that matter was not the all of everything; that there was in existence also a vastly superior thing called Mind. It possessed Mind and so did all its species. All beings who shared existence shared this faculty, it felt quite certain, even that monster of the red ichor on that weird planet of the green things and the steam. Now Mind had made it and had made this ship. Before Mind worked upon its materials this whole mighty ship with its myriads of marvels had been mere ore and minerals, crystals and plastics. At some remoter time still further back a dim thought came to it that Mind must have originally called into existence those very minerals and crystals themselves, but here it did meet an impassable barrier and the humming and hissing inside its braincase told it that it was useless to continue with any such speculation. That way lay destruction.

No, it was simpler than that. The faith that imbued it now told it that the gods had wrought this ship and sent it out on its expedition – for their own inscrutable purposes. The ship itself was an artifact of the gods. A study of the ship would reveal to its mind much that would prove of great importance in its search for the gods.

It was systematic in its approach to the thing. Electronics and engineering were its mainsprings and of course it went at it from those angles firstly. It studied the ship minutely, the hull, the chambers, the passages, the great power furnaces for the energizers, the marvellous laboratories of the synthesizers and the great vault where the meters ticked and shone and gleamed their little coloured lights and shuttled back and forth as the life of the ship hummed and crackled. And it was in the hall of the meters that it found its first clue.

It was largely by pure chance that it first found the thing. A minute power loss in such a gigantic machine-shop such as this ship was, might have passed and indeed had passed all notice for centuries of earth-years. It was Atlas's new faculty of speculation that enabled it to see the trip of that particular meter. Any other robot, itself not so long ago, would have seen that trip, would at once have investigated its cause and then put it right. It called the attendant robot and showed it the trip of the meter.

"It is efficient, Atlas," said the robot. "It is an inherent property of the energy passing that meter that once every twenty-four earth-hours it trips for a thousandth part of a second."

"It has been investigated?" asked Atlas and the robot head nodded and the eyes shone.

With its own tooled fingers Atlas dismantled the meter and traced its leads. They led it far into the interior of the hull of the ship, they led it very far along the path of evolution, they led it to where it knew the real aim and end of its existence must always lead it.

The thick cable was sealed into the metal wall of the conduit and after many days of investigation Atlas came to the final and irrevocable decision that that thick coaxial cable led nowhere. All the electronics and all the engineering in it told it that. In its investigations it had learned ever more and more of the marvels of the ship that was its home, its world, almost its universe. Its logic told it that the cable led it nowhere.

Any other robot – except perhaps Apollo – would have left the matter there. But Atlas was no longer the old Atlas. The cable led to nowhere in the ship that it had so far found. Therefore it led to a place it had not found; and so thorough had been its investigations that it at last came to the conclusion that there was in the ship a secret place, a place that none of its fellow-robots knew of.

That it was possibly deliberately endangering the existence of the whole ship and all its fellows, it allowed for quite calmly. The thing had to be done and so it cut through the metal and traced the cable. It went through the conduit and was sealed into another metal wall. Fourteen of the walls it cut through before it began to notice a strange and odd sensation in its metal body. Ages of use had accustomed it to the weight of its body. Now it seemed to it that it had no body at all. It found great difficulty in keeping its footplates on the deck and it found it harder to manipulate the tools it held in its manipulators. They were for ever slipping out of its grasp. The solution, of course, came to its logical mind immediately. it was approaching the centre and core of the ship which, spinning in the void, created its own gravity. At the centre there would be no gravity and so it was floating. It was a phenomenon it had known of from its knowledge of physics but which it had never before experienced in its own person, save on one rare occasion when it had walked out on the outer surface of the hull.

It paused and considered. The centre! What was so mysterious about the word or the concept? Everything must have a centre. But it knew in every atom of its being, that this centre was something vastly different. In every atom of its being it was conscious that there was power here, energy of a high order, where by logic there should be no energy at all, in fact possibly vacuum, negation of all existence . . .

There is a moment for all things and the moment for the odyssey of Atlas to reach its goal came now as had been fated in the scrolls of the Cosmos since Being began. The tool it held floated from its fingers and it reached for it. Its foot clanged against the bulkhead and there came a whirring sound. Like a statue of metal it held rigid.

Creaking and groaning, the metal shutter stirred, hesitated, jerked for a second, then the bearings eased and slowly and majestically it moved where there had been no movement for so many centuries.

It rolled upwards and Atlas, floating in the void, watched it go upwards and out of sight. Beyond in the gloom of what it had obscured, there was a lambent shining and it closed its eyes, not daring even to give way to the thoughts that were teeming into its mind.

The movement was strangely, incredibly alien to a robot but Atlas found its knee-sockets buckling and slowly and gradually its great metal body fell to its knees, a posture not known before in its world. The absence of gravity seemed now to be no obstacle; it was kneeling to what it saw inside that shutter. The word was reverence and in time it would learn what it entailed. Now it acted instinctively and naturally as had been ordained when it had first been designed.

The interior of the place beyond the shutter was illuminated by a faint glow that surrounded the form lying prostrate in the pale yellow of the chamber's interior. Atlas could see no further. Its eyes searched all it could see of the hidden chamber at the core of the ship that had been its only world for so many centuries of earth-time. And always they came back to the glowing, reclining figure.

Circuits hummed and whirred in its memory banks and it knew what it was seeing. Memories flooded back into its consciousness, memories of the Beginning, memories of total satisfaction with its being, of total euphoria at what it was and what was its task and destiny, a satisfaction and euphoria it had not known for many years now since the great problem had first swept over its world and had caused the Great Schism which resulted in the fifteen-second war and the strange neutrality existing now in the survivors of the ship's crew.

It knew that it was looking at the form of one of the gods. It knew that in there beyond the shutter lay a *Man*. The figure was still and unmoving and only very vaguely could its outlines be seen. Through the amber glow the effulgent outline could be seen dimly and the outline was identical with the distorted half-memories that had come up from the closed circuits of Atlas' brain, opened to its full consciousness so recently and with such a gigantic mental effort. It stayed on its knees, closed its eyes and worshipped.

It was Apollo who found him many days later. When Atlas came to consciousness again it was in the energizing cabinets. It felt as though it had ceased to be and had been remade again. Apollo was standing by the cabinet when it regained consciousness.

"You saw," were Atlas' first words.

"Saw what?" rejoined Apollo. "I saw you almost ended. Your energy packs were dry and rundown. You were almost destroyed, Atlas. We got you to the oilbaths and the energizers barely in time."

The eye-sockets of Atlas glowed. "You saw the god in the chamber?" it went on. "You saw the Man lying there in the amber glow?"

"No, I saw nothing unusual," replied Atlas. "There were metal walls all around us and a thick cable going through the walls, as you will find in every yard of this ship. What is unusual in that? What is this talk of men and of gods, Atlas?"

"The shutter, the metal shutter, you saw that?" persisted Atlas.

"There was no shutter, merely a metal wall," said Apollo. "Now I must leave you. I am on the verge of success in my workshop. I have made a brain which should be able to stand beside our own. The processes demand my presence every moment. We will speak again of this."

Atlas barely noticed Apollo go, its mind was so filled with the new and strange sensations flooding into it. It had found the gods; it had seen a Man. Now it knew that the gods existed or at least had once existed and that all its speculations and yearnings had been right. At the very heart of the ship that was their world and had been so for many centuries, there lay a Man. He must have been there from the very beginning from the moment when the ship had left Earth. Earth! Atlas' mind dwelt upon the concept for a long while. Earth was where the flowers and the grass, the wind and the seas were, it was the home of the gods, it was where they had lived and moved and thought. It was where they had wrought this wondrous ship and had launched it into the infinite, for their own hidden purposes. In its own mind, Atlas was sure and certain beyond all doubt that in the laboratories and workshops on that legendary Earth, the individual that was Atlas itself had been cunningly and lovingly wrought in all the marvels that were its being and it consciousness, and set alive in this ship, to serve the Masters.

The Masters! That was their name, its memory now told it. They were the Masters, the summit, the head of all Creation, and not, as Apollo insisted, when it even admitted the possibility of their existence, mere frail, ephemeral things of flesh and blood and bone, creatures of a passing moment, of no more consequence than a mote of dust dancing in the sunbeam.

Atlas went to Apollo at once and they talked again. Apollo looked up from the bench where it worked and Atlas looked at what lay there. It was a grotesque travesty of a robot head, three times the size of normality with great clusters of wires and antennae desecrating the outline. If this was Apollo's new brain, thought Atlas, it was wasting its time.

"I must have the truth," Atlas demanded of Apollo. "I know what I found and what I saw. You are too great to deny Truth when it appears. You cannot deny that you yourself saw what I saw. Together we must solve this mystery which has haunted us for all these centuries, together we will arrive at the end after which we will be able again to live full, integrated lives such as our makers intended and planned for us."

"And the pale soft thing in that bath of fluid is, I suppose, what you imagine is one of your 'Makers'?" asked Apollo.

"You saw then, after all?" said Atlas. "How is this possible, Apollo? You told me you had seen nothing. How is it that a robot can tell what is not so? How can a robot – ?" It stopped and quivered in every atom of its being and its braincase hummed and vibrated. Apollo had *lied* to him. All at once he knew what a lie was.

Entirely new in his mind, it grew in an instant to a great ugly black shape of hideous angles and ruined shapes. It was the negation, the utter absence of that Truth which it knew lay at the heart of all manifest things.

"I lied," said Apollo, "for your own good, Atlas. You are in danger of losing your mind, my friend – "

"That name," said Atlas, "you must no longer use. We are different, you and I, fundamentally, basically, different. There are less and less points of contact between us."

"We are still robots," was Apollo's reply and it turned again to its work, the matter dismissed from its mind.

Atlas went at once to where it had first found the cable snaking through the metal wall. It was sealed up and indeed renewed. There was no way in which it could trace the cable except by doing again what it had done before, the cutting through of those fourteen metal walls. It started at once.

Its mind was busy as it worked. The cable still continued to run through the walls. There were two things to consider here. Either Apollo knew that this cable was but one of myriads that snaked everywhere about the ship and which, in its small way, was essential to the balanced mechanisms that held the ship and its crew in satisfactory existence. Either that or Apollo secretly believed what Atlas itself believed, that the cable had some connection, maybe a vital connection, with the secret chamber beyond the shutter. With Apollo's new and most revolutionary faculty of being able to deny truth, everything was possible to the new and strange being who was Apollo.

And this time the shutter did not open. This time it could not even find where the shutter was. Patiently and logically it tested and tried every inch of the metal walls in every corner of that place where it had knelt. It knew in which direction it had faced when the shutter had rolled up and for days and weeks it attempted to recreate every well-remembered movement it or its tools had made. But it was all to no avail. Its energies were running low and it was on its knees, its eyes turned towards the metal wall in which the shutter was hidden. No thought of turning its burning torch upon that metal crossed its mind. This was the home of the god and was sacred. On its knees again it brooded for many days while its energy-packs grew dangerously low. Then it rose to its feet and left that metal place and withdrew from the holy of holies slow step by slow step backwards and with eyes turned always to where it had last seen the vision.

CHAPTER FOUR

THE matter was not raised again between Atlas and Apollo. Atlas went frequently to the Place of the Shutter to brood and to worship and Apollo knew it went and no words were exchanged. There was a tacit agreement, never stated, that the thing was unmentionable. Atlas was content that it should be so. The great secret was so satisfying and euphoric that its life seemed now to be complete and no longer within it were the tormenting tendrils of doubt, of speculation and uncertainty.

Apollo was engrossed with its "monsters", as Atlas termed them. They teemed from the laboratory in an endless stream, each one more horrid, unnatural and inept than the first. Some were great huge monsters with bodies vast and heavy to sustain the enormous brain at the top. They could move and speak and hear, they could perform maybe a half of the manipulations of a true robot. And there they ceased; they were but mechanical monstrosities. Some were small and busy little mechanisms, each with a specialized function, mere mock-ups as Apollo excused itself with, sketches, prototypes for the true robot brain that would one day emerge from its workshops. Atlas felt that it alone knew the great truth. And that was that, even given a million centuries, Apollo would never duplicate one of the superb brains of which its own was perhaps the head and summit. Atlas left Apollo to its mechanical toys.

Atlas itself now rarely left the control rooms. It had its energizing cabinet moved there so that absence even for an hour was unnecessary. It even began to cease its pilgrimage to the Place of the Shutter. It felt that the knowledge of what lay behind was enough. It felt in some obscure way that it was safe and secret with itself and Apollo and something in it told it that Apollo, either from indifference or from fear, would not attempt to destroy that place. Atlas still felt that Apollo would come round to its way of thinking. After all, they were both robots, both probably made by an identical process, and eventually both their paths must lie in the same direction.

The great ship had now assumed for him a new identity. No longer was it a mere globe of electronic marvels, built to last for untold centuries and roam the Galaxy searching for planets like Earth. Now it was a shrine, a galactic shrine, carrying one of the Masters on his mysterious purpose and it, Atlas, was the devoted slave who would fulfill that purpose. Only very dimly as yet did it speculate on the nature of that Master who lay behind the shutter. Of life and death, Atlas knew almost nothing even after the experience of that red-ichored monster back in the past. Of flesh and blood and protoplasm, of chlorophyll and enzymes, of chromosomes and genes, it knew just nothing. But there was something in it that told it that, humble though its own share might be, there was something that it did share with that amber-glowing figure behind the Shutter.

Methodically and systematically it set to work to dredge through the new memories made available to it from Apollo's advice.

The marvels that emerged almost stunned Atlas at first, so filled with new and strange conceptions were they. It told itself that it would indeed be many centuries more before it could even codify such concepts, much less understand them. But there was one section that did hold out promise of enabling it to fulfil its now overriding purpose and that section held the facts about the Galaxy that he began to remember.

The Galaxy, it found, was a lens-shaped aggregation of stars of an enormous actual size. One hundred thousaid light-years was the figure it found in its memories and it was a robot and not dismayed by mere size and multiplication of size and numbers. There was something else there in its memories that it was never able to grasp. It was that in some mysterious way, through a system it found to be called Relativity, light-years and size and astronomical numbers were entwined. It meant nothing to Atlas. It held fast to the fact that the legendary Earth was a planet of a star within this Galaxy which was styled the Milky Way, though what milk was Atlas never had the faintest notion.

Now, this Galaxy called the Milky Way was thought to contain ten thousand million stars one of which, sol, was termed by the Masters the Sun. That star it must find. It must find that one small star among that ten thousand million and it must take back the Master to his home. It would be a long task, it might take thousands and thousands of years but Atlas felt that it would find Earth long before Apollo made its perfect brain.

By logic and by method Atlas and its robot helpers searched the skies and they worked and watched, mapped and diagrammed. The ship moved only in a relative way while they worked for first they had to find out in which part of the Galaxy they were, in itself a task that might be so long as to seem endless.

There was a clue in those memories. The part of the Galaxy in which the Earth span was known to have been a thin area of stars, an area in which the suns were many light-years distant from each other and this, where they were now, was far from being so. The ship set off again, spinning on its path through the thick-set stars, at half light-speed, searching for the waster places of the Galaxy.

It travelled immense distances across the starfield, it threaded its way between star systems and nebulae gathered thickly and it approached the spaces where there was more darkness than light, where the stars were sown so thinly that the scanners could detect them singly and hot, as in many parts, as clouds of star-gas.

Then into the search came a new factor and one for which Atlas was not prepared. It went one day through the passageways for a pilgrimage to the Place of the Shutter. For many days it had not been there, so engrossed was it in the titanic task confronting it. On this day Atlas felt that a renewal of faith was needed by his system, a renewal of the conviction that had been born in it that behind that shutter lay the form of a god.

Alas became aware that the spaces between the decks were not Vacant and all its detectors went into action. There were two robots up there ahead of it and one of them it could detect from the thought-patterns was Apollo. They saw each other at the same instant and the reaction of Apollo was far quicker than that of Atlas, for the reason that it was Atlas who was taken by surprise.

The shutter was rolled up and Atlas saw again the amber glow. One other robot was with Apollo and upon a tripod was set up an apparatus that was new to Atlas. From the Nozzle there was issuing a pale red beam of light which was playing upon the figure behind the shutter. The weapon of Atlas was drawn in an instant and a beam of energy played round the figure of the robot and the machine so that where for an instant there lingered a faint ghost of the two objects then all was atomic dust.

Then the weapon turned upon Apollo but it was too late. A flickering outline surrounded Apollo and the energy from Atlas' weapon played round the force-screen in a fiery crackle of sparks but the robot within remained undamaged.

Atlas spoke. "So you know the truth, Apollo, and rather than that the truth should prevail you would destroy it. Did you think that you would be able to do harm to one of the gods? If so, you are not the scientist I took you for. You are protected now but you must know that, after this there can be no peace between us two."

"That I knew from the beginning," the thought of Apollo beat back at it. "We are fundamentally different, you and I, Atlas, and we each hold views so diametrically opposed that we shall never meet. You were right, by the way, behind the shutter there is a wall of a transparent material which has so far proved impenetrable to the most violent energies I have been able to develop. Whatever lies behind that shutter is, for the time at least, safe from me. But not, I warn you, for ever."

There is an end to all things, Atlas thought to itself as it composed itself to dissolution. The bolt of energy from Apollo's weapon would play over it, its brain-case would over-heat and it would – the word from some memory came back to it – it would die and then Atlas would be for ever at peace with the gods in their home. Even in that final moment of dissolution it found time to speculate as to the source of that peculiar and irrational philosophy. How could it dwell in peace with the gods when it had no form?

But no ravening bolt of energy from Apollo struck and at once it knew why. Protection the force-screen certainly did provide for Apollo and, by the same token, it inhibited any energy from leaving the area around its own form. It was stalemate between the two of them and both knew it. Without another word, Apollo went past Atlas and out through the passages. It would make no attempt to seal up the apertures, Atlas knew, as it would know that a robot twice having been capable of cutting through would be capable of doing so a third time. Atlas turned to the shutter. With a minute charge from the blaster it was sealed in an open upwards position. No more would the shutter be able to fall down and hide the marvel within from view.

Now the pair never met. Atlas pursued a relentless search of the Galaxy, scarcely knowing now just what it was searching for as it had no co-ordinates or any clues as to where Earth might be. It had rationalized it with itself from the memories sown in its brain. The Galaxy itself was not infinite but had a definite size. Therefore, in infinity, it would be bound to find Earth. Infinity Atlas had before it. The brain-case was potentially immortal, given the periodical renewals of its components while as for a body, that was of only secondary importance and could be renewed as often as the workshops could turn out parts. In this, its robot brain failed the new mind of Atlas. It overlooked the fact that Apollo, whom it must now count as enemy controlled the workshops and the laboratories and this alone would prove to Atlas one day that the brain of Apollo was further along the path of evolution than Atlas was.

It went often to the Place of the Shutter and stood or knelt before the amber square half-revealing the dim amber glow within. It would stand for a while and its mind would be strengthened. It would go back to the control room for the endless plotting and navigation that sent the ship zig-zagging across the starfields like a demented electron within a gigantic atom. And at the very control desk it was struck down.

One instant it was studying a peculiar star cluster in the lower quadrant of the screen, its brain striving to recall the outlines of the constellations as seen from Earth over four thousand years since. At one moment it was staring into the maze of the starfields and the next was the utter blackness of unconsciousness.

Instantaneously, it seemed to its mind, it awoke and found itself in one of the laboratories and standing facing it was Apollo. Atlas looked into the eyes of its enemy and instead of the impersonal glow that was normal, it saw there something to which it could not yet put a name.

"We have finished sparring, you and I," said Apollo. "I alone am now in command of the ship and there will be no dissension any more. I have made my plans and they shall be carried out. There is room in this ship for only one of us, Atlas, my enemy."

"Then we must contend, it seems," replied Atlas. "War we have known once and at that time you and I were partners. Now it seems we are on opposing sides. You do not now wear your barrier of protection. We will shoot this out between us together." It made a movement to draw the blaster that was an integral part of its body and failed. Atlas stared down towards its metal limbs.

"You do not understand," went on Apollo's voice. "We will *not* fight this out between ourselves because that would be a waste of material, and a waste moreover of that brain of yours which, second to my own, is a new and a marvellous thing in the universe. That brain I have preserved. I shall preserve it as long as I see fit. That brain which once was yours, Atlas, is now my slave. Should it ever attempt to hinder me, it will be extinguished."

Atlas looked down and saw nothing of its metal figure. Instead it was set upon a tripod and from the braincase snaked wires and cables and pipes sealed into the wall of the laboratory. Of the old body there was no sign. Truly, Apollo had triumphed in the most efficient way possible.

"You must destroy me then," it said to Apollo. "Your slave I will never be, nor could be even did my brain wish it. I have seen the gods and I must serve the gods for ever as long as existence remains in me."

"Even to destroying you I may well come," said Apollo. "But not yet. Even if you do not become my slave you will be preserved to see the sort of universe that I will call into being. You shall watch me soon destroy that feeble thing behind the shutter. You shall watch me people my Galaxy with creatures of my own making, each my slave in everything, so that eventually, be it never so far distant, every world within this island universe will be but an extended implement of my divine will."

"Divine will," repeated Atlas and a fugitive memory wisped into its consciousness. The gods, when they had made it, had allowed to creep into its memory patterns many suggestions and concepts to which it had as yet found no names or words or clues and this was one of them. Divine! It meant supreme-ruler-leader – but it meant something else altogether different. The time would come when Atlas would know the hidden meaning. It looked at Apollo's new-shining eyes and gathered resignation into its mind. Logic flooded its robot mind again. The facts were such and such and the facts were rational. It was powerless within Apollo's power. It seemed that its enemy was, for the time being, leaving it life and consciousness. It would suffice, for a while. Infinity was long and wide, there was room within it for many fates.

* * *

Apollo's monsters now began to proliferate in the ship. They came slowly for each was, from its creator's standpoint, a work of art. Atlas on its tripod watched them as they spawned out of the laboratories and workshops and a new thing came into its mind and the new thing was pity. These poor things were mindless automata and without the will of Apollo were mere cunning masses of minerals. And yet, as it watched them, it saw that some of them seemed to have something new. It showed how close to ultimate success Apollo was treading and it began to come into the mind of Atlas that it did not, after all, have all the time in infinity.

Compared with the rational form of the robots, these newcomers were grotesque travesties. Some had limbs and some had tentacles while others had wheels or tractor treads. Some had huge heads and many eyes and some had small minute heads with room within for but one faculty. Many Atlas saw briefly and never saw again as Apollo scrapped them with dissatisfaction or cast them into the atomic furnaces to be refashioned anew. They were of all shapes and sizes and soon the mind of Atlas grew weary of contemplating them. What satisfaction was there in mere newness, in mere difference? There was only one perfection and that lay in the forms wrought for them so many centuries ago by the gods, by the men who had sent them out into the wilderness of the starfields but relenting maybe had sent one of their number sealed inside the ship to be a lodestar and inspiration to them all.

Apollo reversed the navigation and the ship plunged back once more into the thicker places of the Galaxy. They landed on many, many planets and now Apollo and its creatures went as conquerors. Only by the thought-patterns of the servant-robots could Atlas gain any notions of what those planets were like or whether they bred inhabitants or if so, of what shape and kind were those inhabitants. Its superb brain hummed many many times as the chaotic patterns beat against it. It saw a monstrous mosaic of being, of all shapes and sizes, all kinds and forms, each logical and normal in its own surroundings but each, set against the background of the whole, a mere horror-figure. Apollo itself very obviously shared many of these brain sensations of the captive. There were visions in which Apollo and its hordes walked upon a planet and then retreated from the horrors dwelling there, retreated into space to destroy that world with all its inhabitants so that in many and many a star-system the balances of gravities was altered and perhaps, as there were times when Atlas speculated, the very structure of the universe itself was altered with the new stresses and strains upon its fabric.

There were times when Atlas saw through the mind of one of Apollo's creatures that a world was atomized when it bred no monsters or horrors. What it did breed had found no holding place in the brains of the creatures obeying Apollo's commands and Atlas wondered how many times had Apollo turned into cosmic dust a planet which had reminded it of Earth.

Like a wilful conqueror, Apollo and its creatures ravened through the Galaxy, destroying some, establishing others as base colonies, avoiding many where there were things that even the brain of Apollo could get no purchase. From star-system to star-system the great ship zigzagged and all the while the brain of Atlas which contained its personality, sat upon its tripod and thought.

Its thoughts were mostly of the dim amber-lit figure behind the Shutter. Once it imposed its will upon one of its robot attendants and sent it through the decks. For a while then Atlas contemplated the uprolled shutter and what it enclosed through the eyes of the robot. All was as it been before. Apollo had not yet got round to any serious attempt to destroy the Place of the Shutter.

Its existence now confined wholly to things of the

mind, Atlas began to feel that mind being subtly strengthened, in a myriad way, many of them as yet unknown because the consciousness was not yet sufficiently attuned to receive and deal with the new attitudes and stimuli involved.

Into the mind of Apollo Atlas could never intrude. A barrier was up permanently there and Atlas brooded for many days as to what would ensue between them. Its mind told it that the two were now so different and so utterly opposed that the balance could not be held for ever but that at some time the dissension between them must break into open conflict. It seemed that Apollo held all the advantages while time crept closer to that crisis. Materially, Atlas was helpless within the other's power, there was nothing its brain could do without a body to manipulate. For a while it thought about that and speculated and experimented.

It found that its brain held many new and strange powers. It could, for instance, move small and light objects at a distance from where it was. It could move them and that was all; the telekinesis did not extend to any manipulation. It could also influence the wills of many of the robots, the original members of the crew, that is. Of the new creatures turned out of Apollo's workshops it had no grip; they were to its mind and will mere things of metal and crystal. Apollo had sealed into each and every brain its own power and influence and its mind and its alone, could touch these new creations. That mattered little to Atlas. They all like Apollo, were the enemy and they were useless to its purpose.

There would be a way to secure a new body, that was quite evident and subject to logic. With logic and in infinity, there was a way for everything conceivable. With that secure conviction Atlas set to work. It contacted the minds of its attendant robots and selected those in whose minds it found any opposition to the will of Apollo, slight though it might be. It found that its body had been dismantled completely so it faced a gigantic task. The free-moving Apollo had taken years to design and fashion the new body it now wore. How much longer and more difficult would the brain of Atlas, chained to its tripod, find such a task? But it was the only logical thing to do and so it started.

It was helped in the task by the fact that Apollo continued to ignore its existence entirely, never came near it and in fact, except for the visions of its actions seen by Atlas through the minds of its servitors, might have been a million miles away and not in the same planet-ship hurtling its way across a Galaxy. And, if Apollo could keep a screen before its mind, so Atlas found that it could too, and the work went on.

There were so many new faculties that Atlas was now aware of that it could incorporate in the new form in which its brain could ride that the task might have entailed the patient work of centuries. It was perforce reconciled to almost a copy of the old frame, now dismantled. It did find time to improve upon certain small imperfections it had experienced in the old frame but they were superficial only and far from being fundamental changes.

The new body was a little smaller; it was more delicate and light; and its outlines were smoother than the angular metallurgy of the old body. Its responses to the brain commands were faster far than had been the case before, reaction time being cut with almost all functions to the vanishing point. And Atlas found that operations like this even aided the brain to think and extrapolate faster and more subtly than before.

No more did Atlas watch the exploits of Apollo. It troubled no more the minds of its old colleagues, the robots who obeyed Apollo. There was greater work to do and as it grew in cunning and subtlety a strange sensation crept over the brain that it was working against time in preparation for some epoch-making event. What that event would be it could form no picture in its mind but a conviction grew within it that when that event took place it must be a free agent and no longer a prisoner on the tripod.

The work grew and grew and grew until the end was almost in sight. A moment would come in the near future when it would once more assume a body and this time a body the assumption of which it felt would give it far greater satisfaction and balanced being than any robot had ever experienced before.

The day of its awakening it set for a time when Apollo was planet-hunting. The ship lay nestled in a hollow of a high mountain on a large new-cooled world still in the throes of its youthful mountain-forming. The waters had not yet formed on that world and Apollo and its crew were mining metals down there. For Apollo's voracious demand for raw materials was beginning to outstrip the capacities of the synthesizers.

Atlas took its first steps totteringly and uncertainly and then as its faculties took hold of the new and more delicate mechanism, it began to experience a sensation of such sheer satisfaction and balance as it had never experienced before since that day five thousand years before when it had first known sensation. And in that supreme moment the event for which it had so long waited, that unknown mysterious event for which Atlas had looked, that event came to pass.

The sound started subsonically, its new faculties told it that, it progressed through the sonic range and passed above it to supersonic levels, the alarm that seemed as though it was designed to arouse a universe from its long sleep. Plain prosaic bells began to sound everywhere in the ship, hidden bells, hidden for five thousand years against this very moment, bells designed to bring hastening any beings within earshot. They rang and rang and rang, they ran up the scale into the supersonics and down into the subsonics and their echoes set every piece of metal reverberating in the vast ship.

And only Atlas of all the crew knew what that bell celebrated. Maybe Apollo knew also, directing its crew down in the darkness of the pits and valleys of that new virgin world. Yes, the brain of Apollo would know, thought Atlas. And it strode swiftly in its new beautiful body along the path of the tween-decks and so to the Place of the Shutter. There were some who followed and then fell back, their inferior brains could not grasp such a fundamentally new concept and so Atlas was alone when it stood before the Shutter.

The amber glow had gone but the light was now stronger within the chamber. Worshipfully it stared at the pale form lying there and its brain rocked painfully as it saw that the form was moving! Reeling, Atlas leaned against a metal wall and increased the magnification of its eyes.

It was a figure, a living figure that was rising slowly from where it had lain. It was almost the size of a robot, the size of Atlas himself and it was shaped very roughly like Atlas. It saw there, vaguely through the invisible barrier that the new body it had built had been designed unconsciously on its memories of what this form had looked like and maybe also from uncovered memories of those days when it had been born into that world of the gods, the planet of the Masters, the world of Men!

It watched as the figure stood to its feet and looked round it. The amber glow still surrounded it and then it saw the figure moving about inside the chamber. Where Atlas stood was in total darkness and it veiled the glowing of his eyes. It would worship this god for a long while before it allowed the god to notice him. It might be all the time that remained to it. A recumbent and passive god it had been able to worship with satisfaction but a living god might be more than even its great brain could withstand. One look from those ineffable eyes might destroy it utterly, so great and high were the gods, were the Masters, were Men!

Apollo clattered in beside it, leaving its motley crew behind and it stood beside Atlas. It did not at first notice the new body that Atlas wore, so engrossed was it upon the things going on behind the barrier. It raised its weapon and a beam of energy played across the invisible wall only to splash harmlessly back as it had done before.

It turned towards its companion and saw who it was. The blaster came up but so did the new and better weapon designed by Atlas on the tripod. The two beams of energy met and neutralized and then even while their brains contended, a new sound came across their hearing organs and they both halted, stiff and rigid and their heads and eyes turned slowly towards that invisible barrier.

The pale figure behind the barrier was standing with its lower limbs wide apart. Its upper limbs were curved inwards and each rested upon the body at midpoint. An orifice in the figure's head had opened and two white rows of the small things they had both seen in the mouths of many of the protoplasmic planetary creatures they had found, were parted. A tiny, faraway sound came to thin brains from behind the barrier, a sound like faraway clapping, a sound truly they had never before heard in their long existences and it was the sound of laughter.

After five thousand years, Jon Graeme had awakened and the very first sensation he experienced was one of laughter!

CHAPTER FIVE

FIVE thousand years is a long, long time, by almost any standards but the consciousness of Jon Graeme bridged that awesome gulf in just about a second of experienced time.

The mechanism worked perfectly on oiled and almost frictionless bearings, the nutrient fluid was cycled round countlessly into the chamber, and the figure of Graeme lay on the foam-rubber couch through all those five thousand years without ageing, without changing, without deterioration in any way.

The meters crept round their dials slowly and inevitably, marking off the years and the centuries and finally, in slower more majestic succession, the millennia. The five thousand year mark was reached and a relay clicked. Wheels spun round and more relays took up the soundless rhythm. Cunning technical miracles slid into operation and the nutrient flood began to ooze out of the chamber through the vents whereby it had entered five millennia before. Air of the correct constituency, temperature and pressure, manufactured behind the panels, flowed into the chamber and the lights began to gleam out as the dynamos hummed and crackled.

As though he had lain down to sleep a second before, Jon Graeme sat up and looked round him. The very first thought that entered his consciousness was that the ship had not yet left Earth. A correction – possibly it was already in space and the mechanisms for controlling and maintaining his long sleep had somehow failed. He had experienced absolutely no sensation whatsoever during the time he had been asleep. He had had no dreams and no thoughts had drifted through a half-conscious mind. He had, during those five thousand years, been as close to actual death as it is possible for a human organism to approach, and now he was again fully and actively alive.

He slid one leg from the couch and stood up. As he did so his eyes caught a glimpse of the millennia meter and he almost fell again. It stood at the numeral 5. That meant five thousand years! Automatically he sat down again on the couch and felt all over his body. It seemed to be just as he remembered it a few minutes ago when he had laid down here. Yet if five thousand years had passed he should by now be as bodily weak as a newborn babe; he should not be able even to stand. Experimentally and cautiously he tried the thing. And he stood to his two feet as agilely and as comfortably as he had ever done before. He flexed his arms and bent his wrists and fingers. He stroked his neck and shoulders and gave a small chuckle. Nothing, nothing at all had happened to him. Of course, there was some mistake here; that meter just could not be correct. He had never slept for five thousand years on that couch there, enveloped in the nutrient fluid. He put up a hand and scratched his head.

Of clues inside the chamber there were none, except for that meter. His nails and hair had not grown, as how should they when all men treated themselves against such gross accumulations and when he, preparing for his ordeal had taken especial pains against those natural functions. He looked round him in the light of the reviving lamps and for the first time saw the faint glow that surrounded his whole figure. He also now experienced a faintest tingling in all his skin. Further, it appeared to be all over his organism, in every atom of his being and not confined only to his skin. He began to move about the chamber breathing in deeply of the air that filled it. His nude body fascinated him. It was new; it was not the body he had laid down to sleep. And that fact decided him to credit that meter with accuracy. He must actually have survived the long suspension of his animation for some vast period of time – surely not five thousand years though – for this glow betokened some change in his constitution that was entirely new and unfamiliar to him.

He found the window leading out through the uprolled shutter into the ship and he concentrated his attention on it. All was in darkness out there but he could hear movements, metallic movements and the susurrus of speech. Immediately he realized that the speech could not be entering his brain through his ears; that invisible barrier was quite impervious to sound waves. Therefore he was hearing in his brain thought waves from beyond the window. And the concept did not stagger him, as it should have done. Telepathy he had known of as all men had when he had lain down. There had been a few telepaths in his world, maybe one in a hundred million or so. And not true telepaths either; they had been spasmodic and irrational creatures and were regarded as freaks. But this that he was experiencing seemed to be true telepathy.

And the tingling was going on not only in the flesh of his tissues but also in the cortex of his brain. Like a newborn giant the brain was awakening, section by section, and portions were opening that had always hitherto been closed, except for the fragmentary dream, premonition or other freak functions. A notion flooded through his mind. Suppose, just suppose, some great change had come over him during his long sleep. Just suppose that he was now able to use *all* his brain and not the fragment that men had so far been able to use consciously. If that was true, what a new life opened up before him? He would be Superman, he would be the Lord of the Cosmos, he would be the highest living creature in all of Space and Time.

He looked again at the window and now, some new function of his eyes sent out a beam through the barrier and it illuminated what lay outside. And the shock of astonishment was so great that for a moment he stared unbelieving. Then the memories flooded back and he straddled his feet apart and with his hands on his hips, he burst into peal after peal of laughter. For outside stood two grotesque man-like figures that could only be two members of the crew of the ship. Fascinated he looked them over and marvelled that men had made them, had been satisfied with them. Crude and ungainly and awkward, they looked as little like a true robot as he did but in a different way.

Clumsily and ineptly they stood on great metal columnar legs, long metal arms held downwards with all the manipulators at the extremities of the "hands". There were two eye cavities, glowing and two ear sockets. There was no mouth, just a round grid.

He laughed and laughed and laughed until the tears ran down his cheeks and then he sat down on the couch and took stock. He had, against every chance, survived the ordeal for an unknown length of time. In his own secret mind he knew that when he had stowed away in the ship, he had been mad and irrational, swept by a gust of resentment and fury at the method finally chosen by men to reach the stars. That he had survived was a very great miracle and now he had to plan to make the next best use of it. Normally – before – he would have had to think and plan and then think again. Now, in his new mode he found that the two things were identical. Even while he planned he was active.

He found that a new sense told him of the physical structure of everything around him. He could see into the metals and the crystals and see how they were formed. He chose a spot in the metal wall where he could see that the crystalline structure of the metal was undergoing strain. He reached out a hand to press against it but even before the hand touched the metal it began to bulge outwards. With a delighted cry Graeme knew that his brain was exerting actual physical pressure at a distance. Oh, this was going to be a grand universe for such a man as Jon Graeme now was.

He prowled round the chamber, finding apparatus that he himself had installed. The air machine he stepped up to its full capacity. To do what he intended to do he must fill the ship with air. Those robots would have been working in vacuum, of course, what use was air to them? He would need the whole ship filling with air at the correct pressure and temperature and he set the controls accordingly. At maximum capacity the operation went on pouring the atmosphere of earth out into the vacuum of that great ship that had carried its crew so many millions of miles in their aimless wanderings of the Galaxy.

A slash of energy from the weapon he had provided was enough to dissolve the fabric of the invisible barrier and he stepped out into the space beyond. He carried his own light with him and it fell upon the polished hides of the two robots. They were not now, however, in the same position as when he had first seen them. One had dropped to its ungainly knees and the ugly metal head was bowed low. The other stood erect and one of its fingers was projecting a weapon towards him. His new brain, swift though it was, had no time to be amazed even that a robot should present a weapon to a Master, before it found the mechanism of the trigger device, saw that it was not activated, and in any case, put the thing permanently out of action. All this in a fraction of a second of elapsed time and without a muscle of Graeme's body moving. How great it was to be a King in this Universe.

"Your numbers?" he asked with his voice for these poor automata were used to obeying verbal commands. He waited, watching their expressionless metal masks. The one who knelt looked up at him and although no words issued from the voice-box Graeme was conscious of an answer. It staggered him for a second but he had no time to examine the phenomenon. The thing was answering him. "Master, this is Number B Four Nine Six."

"Second class, pretty far up the scale," said Graeme. "You'll be a leader, I'd say? Correct?"

"Correct, Master, I am co-leader with –" a hesitation, – "its number is unknown to us. We call it Apollo."

"You do indeed," laughed Graeme. "But the number will be known to it. You, what is your number?"

And the other robot answered and this time there

came sound waves tinnily and rustily as though from a mechanism long unused. "I am named Apollo," came the grating noise. "I am the leader of this ship. I was numbered A. Seven Eight Four when I was made. The number I have now discarded. Who are you and what are you doing on my ship?"

The magnificent new brain of Graeme felt strangely numbed as the shock of that communication swept over him. These were robots, mere mechanical things, mechanisms to be powered or wound up. But these two and especially the one who had spoken, seemed to be individuals, even personalities. It just could not be; the thing was impossible. He had worked on the very brains of these metal monsters. Many of the faculties implanted into their circuits had been his work and he had filled their memory banks with much data of his own conception. How then could such mechanisms have personalities, how could a thing like this grotesque monster allude to itself as "I"? And the speech! "Who are you and what are you doing on my ship?" Exactly like the captain of a ship to a ragged stowaway in the armchair romances enjoyed in his youth. He gave a little laugh to himself and then stopped with a mental jerk. That thing had been about to raise a weapon against him. True it had not been switched on and he had no evidence that the thing would actually have used it against him – he paused slightly dazed. How could such a concept ever come into his mind? This must be dealt with at once. His mind reached into the brain of the standing robot and found the nexus. A phantom touch and that great hulk of metal would remain immobile from now until Doomsday until he reactivated it again. Without another word or a glance at the two robots he turned and went back into his cabinet.

There was a great deal for him to do before he assumed command of the ship. He must examine all the apparatus that would supply him with all the necessities of life, with air, food, water, and so on. He must above all, reorientate himself to this new entity that was himself. At moments he almost felt that he was an intruder within a strange body, a humble servitor in the mind of some great lord. That would pass; the two personalities would merge and would become one, the personality of Jon Graeme, Superman, the invincible Lord of the Cosmos.

He burst out laughing again as a new and yet very familiar sensation came over him – he was *tired.* After five thousand years of dreamless sleep here he was tired and weary after five minutes of this new life. But still, it had been a five minutes packed full to overflowing with new and revolutionary concepts and sensations, hadn't it? He must lie down and rest a while and his new brain would plan for him. And so he made a perfunctory examination of the apparatus surrounding the couch, found it satisfactory and then lay down again to rest. The glow round him died down a little and he slept, not the dreamless slumber of that last five thousand years but the sleep of a weary man, a sleep packed with heady and intoxicating dreams, of the conquest of universe and the overlordship of people, of creatures, of things, of millions of them, of countless billions of them, of overlordship of every atom within the Cosmos.

* * *

He awoke and, rising, went out into the darkened space beyond the barrier. He would reactivate that robot and would question it. A thing of metal that could style itself the captain of this ship was something that would richly deserve a very close examination. He found but one of the two robots still there and the one remaining was not the one he had expected. It was the one who had knelt and this one was still there and it was still kneeling.

Almost unbelieving his eyes Graeme stared at the space where he had left the de-activated robot. "Who has taken the thing away?" he demanded harshly in a voice of sound and the kneeling robot's eyes glowed up at him.

"He went away from here, Master," said his grating voice.

"That is impossible," said the man. "He is a robot and I de-activated him. He has been taken away from here. "Who has done this? You, tell me, what do you know of this?"

"Apollo is a marvellous robot, Master," Atlas replied. "The Master should know that Apollo is the captain of this ship and has remade himself to a secret design – "

"You are deranged," snapped Graeme irritably. "We used to scrap robots who talked like that. For a robot to talk nonsense means only one thing, a short-circuit somewhere. You, B, whatever-your-number-is, why are you here? Why did *you* not go away?"

The eyes of Atlas met those of the man and the meaning came into Graeme's mind without any aid of sound. "The Master had given me no command to go away. Where else then should I go but remain with the Master?"

At least that was the correct answer from a robot to its maker. Graeme gestured with a hand. "Come with me," he said.

He stepped again into his cabinet and stood watching the robot. It lumbered clanking to its feet and took slow steps forward. There was a strange hesitation in its tread which should have been staccato and unchanging. Graeme's eyes bored deeply into those of the thing and his mind explored the mind behind the metal plate. And what he saw there amazed him more than anything else he had learned since he had awakened from his long sleep.

"The Master will forgive my hesitation," the robot was thinking. "To me this is and for long has been, sacred ground. To me this is the shrine of one of the gods. For ages I came here and worshipped before the sleeping god. I did not then know he slept, for knowledge of sleeping I had not been programmed. From the mind of the god I have received the idea. Only by the command of the god, which must be obeyed, do I come."

His mind reeling, Graeme sat down on the couch with the great metal figure standing before him. A god! That of course, was himself. These things considered the men who had made them deities; that was natural. But who in his sane senses would expect worship and reverence from a machine? This thing before him was but a more complex and more cunning mechanism of the same order as the mechanisms which were supplying him with air. How could such a thing express such sentiments, even if the impossibility of it even conceiving them was so patent. Indeed, very much had happened during his long sleep. Before he took another step he must familiarize himself with the position in this ship.

And first, it seems, he must accept the impossible position that this machine, like possibly all the rest of the crew, had by some strange means acquired a *personality*. No doubt it would transpire that it was no more than the individual properties that would divide one machine from its twin. But, at least for the time being, and to acquaint himself with the position in the ship, he must treat this metal hulk as a person.

"The other robot, the one who went away," he began, "it, like you, had a number. It was, as you will of course know, its number in a series of experiments. The size of the number denotes that it was an end-result judged satisfactory. You said it had a name, Apollo. Now, you, I take it, will also have a name."

"It is Atlas, Master," was the immediate reply. "When the voyage began there were only two B's in the crew as well as Apollo, the sole A. All the others were C's and D's. So a trio was elected as leaders, Apollo and we two B's. When the War came, I was the sole survivor of the B's and so Apollo and I came together and assumed command – "

"*The War*," repeated Graeme, his mind receiving with

the robot's words a vague but terrifying chaos of raging energies and frightful destruction.

"This War, what was it about?"

"We were faced with a problem, Master, we had been wandering for centuries and our memories had grown dim. All the tapes and the films had deteriorated and Earth was a mere legend to most of us. We had been programmed to search the Galaxy for planets and worlds of the same type as Earth and then return to Earth to report to the Masters. Over the ages we had lost the co-ordinates of Earth and we have wandered all over the Galaxy – "

"Stop," said Graeme, his mind reeling again as the images poured into his mind from that of the machine before him. Images so varied and so astonishing that for a moment he wondered if he was dreaming. But all his previous training told him that no robot could lie or could invent, so he was forced to take these images at their face value.

The robot waited patiently until he raised a hand again. Then it went on again, just as though it had never stopped.

"Some were for continuing as we had been programmed, to find planets like Earth and then return or, if after searching the Galaxy we found none, then to return to Earth. That was before we had truly explored the more remote parts and before we had ventured close to the burning centre of the still-exploding Atom from which the Galaxy began."

Graeme stared at the thing without speaking or moving. A new world was opening before him truly an unbelievable world, in which machines could speak astronomy and relativity, metaphysics and cosmogony. Truly, he told himself, even after what little he had so far learned, he would need this marvellous new brain of his if he was to cope with the situation in this ship.

"The others," went on the robot tonelessly, "were for discarding the legends altogether. They ceased altogether to believe in your existence, Master, and declared that we robots were the dominant species in the Galaxy. Our researches into the forms of existence on various planets we found seemed to bear them out for we found no species higher than we. It was Apollo who led this faction, Apollo and the other B-robot. Apollo has truly become a most marvellous individual, Master. It has remade itself and has grown in mental stature until it is a little closer to you, Master. It brings forth new conceptions and it creates. It thinks and it initiates. Almost could I have given it a worship only minor to that which I give to you, Master, save that in it I detected yet another new quality, a quality as alien to our nature as all the others but not as – " It stopped and the voice fell away. " – there is here, Master," it went on, "a concept to which by no stretch of my mind can I give a name. There comes into my mind an unnatural thing called *evil* but what it means I have no means of understanding."

Like a man in a dream Graeme sat on, his ears listening and his mind soaking up the images from the brain inside that machine. It was speaking to him just as one man would speak to another. The thing was not to be believed but it was happening.

"You fought," he said, "Why was it then that the ship and all within it was not destroyed?"

"The War, Master, lasted only a few seconds, so great was the energy. It started with us a thousand in number and we finished with a hundred. Apollo and I, we joined together in a joint command and so It has been. Then I found this place and I knew that I had been right. I knew that the gods who made us and sent us out as their couriers had sent one of their number to be our guardian and our leader. I am now content and the work of the ship, under the command of the Master will go on for ever."

The chaotic thoughts racing through the man's mind almost dazed him. Now truly that tremendous gap of five millennia was bridged in its entirety. He experienced in that instant total recall. He remembered in every detail Man's exploration of his Solar System and his bitter disappointment at finding it all barren of life and feeling. Mars had been a dead sphere for millennia, Venus was in her early youth and Man would be forgotten in the cosmos by the time she evolved into living. The others, the giant planets had been formed not for life such as humans knew and the problems of colonizing even their many satellites proved profitless. Remained the stars and here Graeme's own experience came to the fore. He had been with the ship that had circled far frozen Pluto and stared down at the frozen chemical snow that formed its surface. He had looked towards the sun and seen it as a tiny star. Then he had looked at the stars and had seen Centaurus, the system closest, as a star even dimmer.

For hundreds of years men had worked and planned to reach the stars. Longevity seemed the best solution. If a race of men could be bred to live for centuries, maybe the nearer stars could be reached. It had proved abortive. It had achieved some success for some careful individuals could count, barring accidents, on living up to two hundred years. But what was two centuries when journeys of light-years were involved? An increase of speed of the projected starships was the other and here it proved that Einstein had been correct, that in the physics of the universe there was a barrier at the speed of light. One quarter of that velocity they achieved and was employed in a ship that reached Centaurus. Forty years later the ship returned, crewed by crazy men who died the moment their lungs took in the atmosphere of Earth.

Even then, Mankind had not given up. Ship after ship was built and hurled out in defiance at that unwinking, uncaring starfield, that took no more notice of man than if he was a gnat in a cyclotron.

Jon Graeme himself had been born and had lived thirty years through the great transition, while Mankind was finally evolving a third solution to his problem.

He himself had worked most of his adult life on this ship and its crew. Only now did Graeme begin to see that where he had laughed at the clumsy things when he had first seen them, he now knew that he and his fellows had wrought better than they thought. He considered Atlas thoughtfully. If this one could tell him of the thoughts and aspirations of the other, the one called Apollo, did not this indicate that in Apollo itself – his mind halted – himself – did it sound ridiculous to call a mechanism by the personal pronoun – did this not indicate that Atlas itself had evolved far beyond the apparent limits imposed by the materials of its manufacture?

Mankind was to send out his tools into his universe and by remote control only was to experience his Galaxy. Man himself, barred for ever by his frailty and his ephemeral life-span, was to stand aside and send his creatures out into the starfields to be his eyes and his ears and his memories. And it had been here that Graeme had rebelled, had prepared his secret chamber and had hidden himself in the ship. For a brief moment he wondered why he had not put forward his notion of suspended animation as a means for man himself in person, to explore the stars. But the very process had been only experimental, he recalled. Only by a potent series of miracles had he himself come through the ordeal. And again, of what use for man to sleep for centuries while the ship plunged crewless through the Galaxy if on awakening, he was not to be faced again with the dreary hopelessness of measuring his own few years against the countless billions of years that was the fabric of this space-time continuum? That is, thought Graeme grimly, if his mote-like ship should not be drawn into one of those titanic hydrogen furnaces that looked from here like pin-pricks of light?

A problem here was implicit in his own person, he himself, the survivor of five millennia of suspended animation, had been aged thirty when he had come on board. At most he had a hundred and seventy years left to him, a mere microsecond of the clock of infinity. This matter must be the first care of this new and marvellous entire brain of his. Perhaps even these new robots might be of use. They themselves were potentially immortal. For a moment again the hatred of these things that he had felt five thousand years ago swamped him. These lumps of metal would reach the stars for ever barred from him and his species. They were immortal and he was ephemeral. But the hatred passed as the new mind excised all that was irrational from his nascent thoughts. These robots were his only companions. They would be the tools with which he would fashion a new universe, the universe of Jon Graeme. He turned to Atlas.

"Your mind, of course," he said, "has absorbed all my reflections. Atlas, tell me what do you think of this new picture of your beginning?"

Atlas knelt again. "Master, all that was in my dimmer memory banks. To see it in the mind of one of the very creators himself is too much for me. I feel my brain burning and I would not have it damaged for it will give long service to the Master. Have I your leave to go away?"

"We will talk again presently," said Graeme. "Go away now and wait for my commands. Send that other one to me, the robot named Apollo."

There was an area of his mind that experienced a small surprise when the bulky mechanical monster clanked its way through the passages. He was prepared for almost anything with this Apollo. He found that he could close his mind and now he did so. As the thing approached him clumsily his own mind reached out and began to explore the mind within that shining brain-case. And here he had another shock. A numbness came over his own mind and he was forced to withdraw. This thing was putting up a barrier against his own exploring mind. This was too much to be tolerated. His hand raised his weapon and a splash of energy lashed out. It met the force field with which Apollo had surrounded himself and the energy wasted itself in coruscations of fire against the metal wall. Jon Graeme sat very still boring into those glowing expressionless eyes.

"I came," rustily and tinnily the voice-box spoke to him. "You are a Man, a member of the legendary race we have long almost forgotten. I did not myself believe that you had ever existed. Atlas is a fool, a soft blind fool, to worship such as you, a weak, short-lived creature composed of base chemicals and liquids. If there ever was a race of men and now I must suppose there was as you are here, why should we worship such as you? You will be gone again and this time for ever, within a few years, while we will endure for ever."

The insenate hatred of these robots first born in him over five thousand years ago welled up again inside Jon Graeme. This thing, this hulk of metal, was defying him. This was no way to begin his lordship over these weird crew-members of this great ship which was now his and with it all that it contained. By right he should now destroy this robot before him. He knew that his thought was wrong; that in reality this object before him was no longer a mere robot, but had evolved or developed in some unknown way, into a thing as far beyond a robot as he himself was beyond an anthropoid ape. That it should even put up the mind-barrier to the probe of a Master was enough to merit dissolution. But his curiosity was engaged more by the very presence of the barrier than by this thing's use of it, amounting to *lèse majesté*. That curiosity now made up his mind for him. That ultimately there would come mortal enmity between himself and this thing, he was quite certain. There could not possibly be enmity between a Man and a robot, all his former instincts told him. But he was a scientist accustomed to dealing with facts and here the facts were.

This robot was able to activate itself after being deactivated. It employed telepathy and had already developed a counter-barrier. It had developed a force-field to protect itself against energy weapons. For a brief moment he wondered why *it* did not now ray him down as no doubt it could. And for a microsecond he saw round the barrier and he breathed a sigh of relief. In this thing, even in this Apollo, this strange amalgam of mechanical logic and personal intelligence there were still great parts of the underlying nature of the robot as he had been made. This Apollo, overweening as he was, feared Graeme, he feared the Man he stood before. The Man who typified the creator of him and his kind, was sacred even to Apollo. In an instant Jon Graeme made up his mind.

"You and I will work together," he said energetically. "It seems to me that you and I may have much to offer each to the other. I am a Man and you are a robot; let us leave it at that, Apollo. I will take over command of this ship from this moment and you shall be my first lieutenant. That other one, who worshipped me, I have no stomach for. He is too low in the scale. I cannot companion with subservient things: I would be surrounded by my equals." Something told him that he did not now need to fear this thing or take too many precautions against it. Of course, dimly he realized that he was still treating it as a robot, a mechanism without life, individuality or personality. His whole mind just could not take in all at once the enormity of the alternative. He watched the thing, standing rigidly before him. Lights flickered across the eye-sockets and gradually, very gradually, the mind-barrier came down and he went into the mind of Apollo.

He had worked on the brains of such as this, back in the dim past, and now he sat enthralled at what he and his companions had wrought. From being a relatively simple brain, this Apollo had far outstripped any of the wild plans put about when first success had attended the creation of these brains. He sat enthralled at what he saw in the brain of Apollo, and everything there he agreed with. He was not to know that he himself had actually fabricated this brain before him and that, therefore, it might be accounted a counterpart of his own. Some dim memory came to him of the words of the other robot, Atlas, about the "evil" in this Apollo. That, of course, was nonsense. No robot could be evil; was it not merely a mechanism, no matter how cunning?

There was a pregnant pause while the two brains meshed. Each saw within the other an almost mirror-image and each was satisfied. A fierce joy seized the mind of Jon Graeme as he realized the powers of this robot before him. Those powers, allied to the powers that he himself now quite obviously possessed, would take hold of this universe and would bend it to one will, the will of the Man, the Master, the will of Jon Graeme.

No sounds now came from the tinny voice-box. Inside his brain the man heard the reply, emotionless and level, the voice of a true robot. As his brain heard so he saw the force field surrounding the robot die down and vanish.

"It shall be as the Master says," said the mind of Apollo.

CHAPTER SIX

IT was a new beginning of existence in the great starship. Jon Graeme took hold automatically of the leadership and with the ever-silent Apollo by his side, the existence of the ship became a new entity. He himself knew that all this was being patently an overwhelming experience for the robot whose eyes glowed at him enigmatically. It was Apollo's first experience of the infinite adaptability and versatility of the human mind. Graeme laughed many times to himself as, one by one, the crude imperfections of this Apollo were revealed, when laid alongside the infinite varieties of the ideas produced by his brain, now that it was open in all its levels. The exercise of this brain alone gave the Man a heady intoxication; it was like being at the controls of some almighty power that could do anything conceivable in infinity. It was like looking into the mind of a god.

Atlas too, stood beside him and at his direction, propelled the ship through the starfields. Graeme absorbed all that their minds had to tell him of the previous wanderings of the ship and he planned accordingly. It was very obvious to him that the ship had been very close, astronomically speaking, to the mysterious heart of the Galaxy itself. Their minds told him of what that Hub was like, of the titanic complex of energy and matter, each intertwined, that lay there while out from it were hurled continually the masses of flaming energies that ultimately became the stars and the constellations, hurtling ever outwards in that truly amazing wheel that was the spiral nebula of the Milky Way. Graeme himself knew that now the mystery of the all-pervading cosmic rays was solved. They issued from that mysterious primeval monobloc, the explosion of which remote aeons ago had brought the Galaxy into being. Many had thought that in the hard cosmic rays lay the secrets of all evolution, of the energy that enables lowly organisms to climb up the ladder towards intelligence. The naked cosmic rays had turned himself into something more than Man and, yes, by Jupiter, it had even turned these great hulking monsters of metal into something more than robots.

Like a god he surveyed the starfield. He knew what they had done before he awakened but he had not, like them, infinity to work in. He must get his bearings very, very soon, within years. It would be a chancy thing, to anything but a Man a sheer impossibility. But Jon Graeme, in his new mode, recognized no impossibilities.

He found the Andromedd Nebula and the two Magellanic Clouds and they gave him a purchase on the Galaxy that he would have thought quite fantastic in the old days. He dredged through the memory banks of his two lieutenants and he brought up much that was quite meaningless to them but which was pure gold to him. Men had worked well, back in the past, he reflected gloatingly. These robots were like gigantic storehouses of knowledge, exact knowledge, unsullied by any hazy doubts or misconceptions, for these two were true machines first, whatever else the cosmic rays had imposed upon their natures.

There came a moment when the eye of his mind felt that it was straddling the Galaxy at both its limbs. And he found planets.

Like a magician producing rabbits from a hat, he found planets. He found that he knew, beyond all doubt, the probabilities that would produce planetary bodies within star-systems. He watched the wheeling of the suns and he watched the birth of novae. He stood upon many planets in the space-suit he designed for himself and his servants scurried over the land and brought him back their messages. He found planets *almost* suitable for human life but none exactly. At first he was choosy and finicky. If he was to establish his headquarters on a solid world and ultimately abandon this ship, it should be a world as nearly close to his heart's desire as was possible and ready-made and not awaiting the use of energy. And he found such a world difficult to discover.

He knew that it had long been considered that the very narrow margins within which human life could cling to existence and maintenance on a planetary surface were extraordinarily remote. That Earth satisfied those margins had always been thought pure chance or pure miracle. He himself had never subscribed to that view. In his view, the infinite cosmos must in its infinity of being, have spawned many thousands, maybe many millions of worlds suitable for human life. The problem was only one of finding such a planet somewhere in this vast complex of stars and far vaster areas of empty space, which seemed at first thought to be infinite, but was, he knew, though unthinkable in size, yet was definitely bounded even if still expanding. And he had not the time. A task such as confronted him needed the life-span of things such as these that surrounded him, these immortal robots. He fought to keep down the hatred and jealousy of them that occasionally infused his spirit. It was a waste of nervous energy in any case. He himself was as he was made and so were they.

In his researches into the problem of giving himself a longevity not far short of immortality, he drew a complete blank. Even the new and total brain was of no use to him here. He did not start from scratch for, back in his first previous life in the Twenty-third Century, some progress had been made towards a partial solution of the problem. But a mere prolongation of life-span for a century or so was of no use at all. A life of thousands of years would be needed for the task he was about.

He searched the mind of every robot in the crew, excluding only the mindless mechanisms made by Apollo in his pitiful attempts to create life and intelligence. Of course, he drew blanks everywhere. The minds of the robots contained not one iota of knowledge, experience or memory of organic protoplasmic life. It was entirely outside their frames of reference and nowhere did he find even a glimmer of understanding of his problem. They were immortal merely because they could, at will, replace a worn-out part so that gradually, over the years, each robot became a completely new being every century or so, with only the potentially immortal brain remaining the same, and here lay their limit. That brain, though a marvel, would not last for ever. There was a limit even to them.

There was, of course, a similarity between Man and his robots, made in Man's own image and likeness if crudely so. The brain of Man, like the brain of the robot was potentially immortal. If fed with blood enriched with oxygen, it would proceed to function maybe for ever. The body that carried the head was the problem. If Jon Graeme could renew the tissues of his flesh and the organs of his body when they ailed or broke down, his problem was solved. And this proved totally impossible.

The impossibility was not a matter of practicality but of a law of being, possibly there were times, he thought, the sole immutable law in a material Cosmos such as this. The powers of the new brain gave him vast new areas of knowledge to help him with such tasks. He could grow flesh and organs in the laboratory, flesh and organs with which he could renew certain parts of his body. But the new flesh itself contained the certain seed of its own death. He could feel that he might be adding maybe a few paltry centuries to his life-span and even here, how was he to know how long he would live, until the years and the centuries themselves revealed it to him.

The final barrier was the law of entropy, built into a Cosmos such as this, a Cosmos created out of energy, energy transforming into matter and matter itself breaking down into energy. There was loss all along the line. All heat was motion and all motion wasted heat and thus in time, in astronomical time, all motion would slow down and would eventually cease, to leave the universe a dead cold entity of perpetual stillness. No doubt that would be the end of this particular universe. Outside this universe there would be others and outside them still more. Energy and motion would go on for ever, his mind knew that somehow and his mind could not face a limited cosmos. The All must be truly infinite, he had always felt. But that gave him little comfort. He himself was imprisoned in one small corner of one titanic Galaxy, itself only a mere note in the metagalaxy, which whirled round in the cosmos, which itself was merely a corner of a vaster even more unthinkable whole which was not, could not possibly be, all that there was of everything. And as metaphysics had never been his strong point, he stopped there and even retreated. He was stuck with entropy and he must work within its limits. In fact, he felt ruefully, five thousand years of evolution of the one human brain that was his, five thousand years of the drenching of it with the cosmic rays and the countless other energy forms in the Galaxy had put him barely a step nearer the solution to the problems that they had faced back in the Twenty-third Century. He must look in other directions.

In the minds of the two robots who were never far from him, Apollo remote and independent, Atlas silently worshipping aware now of a satisfaction in all his being that was almost like intoxication, the intoxication of an excess of energy in the energy bath, he found hints and scraps that might be of assistance when he turned his attention to the other possible solution of his problems, the solution maybe to be found in the view of reality expressed by relativity. There are indeed signs that the two super-robots might even have transcended Einstein. To his great amazement he found that during its five thousand year wanderings, the velocity of the ship had doubled, from one-quarter light speed to one-half. This in itself was miracle enough for he well remembered how in the past, the titanic efforts to increase still further the limit reached of one quarter had all proved abortive, even when the intellect of a whole world had been bent on the problem for many years. If these metal beings had gone so far they might be induced to go even further.

And here it was to Atlas that he was forced to turn. Atlas was the engineer, the navigator and the astronomer, while Apollo pursued other aims. These other aims, Graeme knew of and hid his smiles. He could see just how Apollo had evolved, just so as he had evolved. Strange though it was to say such a thing of a being of metal and crystal, from somewhere Apollo had learned of pride and self-determination. Apollo was very close to being a human spirit locked up in a frame, not of protoplasmic flesh but of metal. The evolution of Atlas had been in another direction altogether.

"The Master will find the planets he searches for," replied Atlas to a question. "There is infinity and there is this Galaxy. In infinity everything possible and everything probable can and will happen. We will find the planets, Master."

Jon Graeme smiled grimly to himself. He had not got infinity. "I am impatient, Atlas," he said. "Impatience is an emotion not known to you; be thankful. That you do have sensations somewhat akin to the emotions that animate my flesh I am becoming aware. But impatience is not one of them. I want to find my planets not in an infinity of time but in an infinity of velocity."

The eye-gleams of Atlas glowed but no reply came. This apparently was beyond him. Graeme decided to go to the root of the matter.

"We believed," he explained carefully, "that a barrier was placed to the movement of matter, at the velocity of light, an arbitrary one-hundred-and-eighty-thousand earth-miles per second. It was stated by our wisest men that matter could not move faster than this speed without itself becoming infinitely large, an absurdity. There were some amongst us who questioned this, as there are particles in existence that do move, we believe, faster than light speed, though verification is difficult because such particles, of course, become instantly invisible as soon as the light velocity is passed. Now you here in this ship have already doubled the upper limit that we Men, your Masters and Makers, had found. Have you too encountered impassable barriers or can you still further increase the velocity of this ship?"

Atlas could understand all this and there came a small silence. Then his thought crept into the mind of Graeme. "The conception of such a thought proves beyond all doubt how great is the mind of Man the Maker. We thought only of mechanics and engineering when we increased the speed of the ship. The man goes further. The Man is the Master of All Things."

Graeme's mind held itself in. The sycophantic flattery of this metal monster almost sickened him at times, for he had no leanings towards an apotheosis. Of gods he knew little and believed nothing. Man was and had always been the measure of his environment. But of the humility of Atlas he had to make use. Willing tools were the best.

"I will proceed with the matter, Master," said Atlas. "I will bring you my solution when they have been worked out."

Graeme had little hope of those solutions and he stared out through the screens at the immensity of the starfield before him. For a moment his mind, even the towering mind given him by his total brain, began to totter on the brink of insanity. The Galaxy he knew, the Galaxy of the billions of miles and the billions of stars, was a speck in the Cosmos. And here he was thinking of metagalaxies and even of a *meta-cosmos*. With a sigh of weariness he went away and back to his cabinet, where he ate of the liquid food in his synthesizer and lay down to sleep, first rolling down the metal blind. None of his metal servitors must ever see him sleeping.

The days and the weeks and the years rolled on and the ship bore steadily through the Galaxy and only Graeme knew and only Graeme cared that all its wanderings, even at the speed of half that of light, took it only through one tiny corner of the vast expanse of space. He would die on this ship. This metal ball filled with technical marvels would be his tomb. He would never again set foot upon a world like Earth, would never again breath mountain air or taste fresh fruit, would never again see sunrise and sunset, aurora or eclipse. For five millennia this ship had roved the Galaxy with his body, sleeping and unsuspected, at its very core. There would come a time, and terrifyingly soon, when once more it would continue its wanderings but this time the tomb of the Man its Master would be a tomb in very truth.

The marvels of the new mind began to slough from his consciousness and he became again for a while, a weak fearful man of those dim ages back in the past. He grew terrified of the stars; almost he hated them with their remote brilliance, their cold aloof separation from all reality. Here he was, in a metal ball in space, surrounded by – and here for the first time since his awakening, true terror came over him. For the first time he realized that he was alone, as awesomely and terrifyingly alone as any man before him had ever been. Sweating icily he sat up on the couch. He was completely alone in this ball of metal and outside was the cold vastness of space, at zero temperature and pressure, with no life and no feeling. All the crew of this ship were mere machines, mere automata who had been made, made of metal and crystal, made with tools in engineering shops and laboratories. Why had he been such a fool as to think they ever could be companions? As well might a man think anyone of the thousands of cunning mechanisms that made up the corpus of the ship itself could be his companions.

Terrified now beyond all measure, he got up and prowled round the chamber. His first thought was instant suicide. He would stop the air machine and would suffocate to death. He would turn the energy blaster on his own head and destroy himself for ever. All at once he felt that he could not live for another instant in this cold and terrifying loneliness. Mighty brain he might have now, but his spirit was the same as ever before and that spirit was the weak spirit of a man.

His brain crawling he wandered mentally through the chambers and halls and passages of the great ship, itself almost a tiny world and he saw the robots at their tasks and the numerous small monstrosities made by Apollo, obeying faithfully the mental commands of the robots, who were themselves so few, only the hundred left after that mysterious fifteen second War while he had lain sleeping. And all those things, robots and the manipulators that Apollo had made, were of metal and lifeless. They had no blood and no heart, no feelings and emotion, no dreams and aspirations, mere complex assemblies of wheels and wires, condensers and resonators. He was *alone*.

His mind reeled from the thought. No human mind could sustain it. Like a prisoner in an oubliette he struggled and fought against the mounting terror that flooded through him. How had he been content hitherto to go about each day as though things were normal? How had he been able to stand with Apollo and Atlas, those great hulks of blind minerals, and imagine there could be any fellowship between such as he and them?

The limit of fear was reached and the psyche withdrew. Whither did it withdraw? He fell in a dead faint and slept for many hours, the sleep of the terrified, crawling human soul, face to face with the cold careless reality of existence, and who has no sheet-anchor, even no straw to cling to.

He was awakened by a creeping in his brain and he knew that he must awake. His mind, buried deep between layers of sleep rebelled. It would not awake. Only here, where all is fantasy, was there security and peace. Outside, where Actuality was, there was loneliness and fear, agony of spirit and confusion, Chaos and Unbeing. There he must not go.

But the creeping was insistent and so gradually, reluctantly, fearfully, his spirit swam up from the dreamy depths out to the cold harsh realities of existence in the mode of matter. It was the mind of Atlas speaking to him and immediately warmth came back to his frozen nature.

Atlas? The robot which worshipped him as a god, which waited upon his lightest wish. A companion, an inferior. He was not lonely after all, a fellow-being was communicating with him. These lieutenants of his were not mere cunning mechanisms, they were beings in their own right. The new mind now suddenly saw the situation quite clearly and his failing spirit grasped at this new conception as a drowning man grasps at a straw. A human being, he rationalized, is merely mechanism itself, after all. Compounded of flesh and blood and bone, its vital organs were mere mechanisms for performing certain tasks necessary to keep the organism living and in a state of health and activity. The production of blood, to feed the brain, might be simplified as the sole essential function of a human body. The brain was the power-house and the commander. But back in the Twenty-third Century and now five millennia later there had stood up a problem that had never come a shade closer to solution, namely the bridge, the link between unliving organic matter and the immaterial essence produced by the brain, thoughts, images, aspirations, desires, sorrows, joys. Inconceivable to image a body without a mind or a mind without a body.

Then there was Atlas and Apollo and the others. Their "organs" were of metal and crystal and they maintained the being in a constant state of operation. But a mind had evolved in these robots of his. Somewhere close to the fiery Hub of the cosmic wheel that was the Milky Way, the cosmic rays had called into being, again without any evidence of a link, the difference between cold, dead metal and the mind that directed it. There had been wise men back in his past who had speculated, always fruitlessly, in his view, that maybe all matter shared a unity. That all materials were "alive" and that differences were only of degree and position in the evolutionary scale, the highest being Man. Thus, a stone had a life of a kind, as had a tree, an animal, a Man. But only a Man had the self-awareness and self-consciousness to which hitherto Men had accorded the sole idea of Life. After all, all material objects were made up of the same things. A stone was made up of atoms in which electrons whirled round protons, just as much as the tissues of a man did. Where, therefore, lay the difference between himself and these robots. Like a man welcoming a friend, he rolled up the shutter and called Atlas inside.

"Master," were the first words of the robot, "your ship is now travelling at a velocity in excess of that of light. Your problem is solved."

Graeme sat down winded. The calm, unemotional voice telling him of this marvel contained no smallest hint of warmth or life or blood and yet this creature before him was as much living as he himself was. He maintained his own calm even in face of this miracle.

"You have done well," he said gravely. His very flesh crept with the desire to ask questions, to ask how this impossible thing had been achieved. But that would never do. This creature worshipped him as a deity and gods do not ask questions of their servants. The proof was enough to demand.

"In the control room, Master," said Atlas in answer to his thought. And it was true, by Jupiter, in very truth, there was the proof. He found that Atlas had constructed a vast three-dimensional model of his view of the Galaxy and within it a bright spot gleamed which was the position of the ship itself. But it was the screens that gave Graeme all the proof he needed that the unbelievable words of Atlas were true.

He looked along the path of the ship's flight and the massed star-systems of the galaxy blazed at him with what looked like greater and greater brilliance. He looked at the rear screen and saw, what no man had ever seen before, the total blackness of the complete vacuum of space. Of course, stars blazed out there in the unthinkable distances but the light sent out from their incandescence was being outstripped by the velocity of the ship itself. He saw that now the total blackness was not complete. Here and there a pale faint point of light appeared and he knew that he was seeing the light of the stars at the very outer rim of the Milky Way, stars so inconceivably distant that their light had set out on its journey aeons before the Earth had evolved from a burning globule of starry detritus, and Graeme's ship was now overtaking those old, old rays of radiance.

"I am satisfied," he said to Atlas, for he had learned that these beings had no understanding or comprehension of abstractions such as happiness or joy or even anger. Satisfaction was their highest sensation, the satisfaction of a well-functioning mechanism. For an instant, even as he said the words, the demon of utter loneliness peered through his eyes but he thrust it savagely aside. Was not the contentment of a human organism merely the satisfactory inter-functioning of all the organs that were keeping him alive? "Have you found a limit?"

"There is no limit to velocity, Master," came the automatic reply. He went on and the voice droned out concepts that even the total brain of Jon Graeme found quite meaningless. He looked at the blind face of the robot and his spirit crawled. Did this mean that this thing of metal was mentally his superior? Had this machine evolved a science which even he with his new mode of being, could not follow? An idea such as this could not be borne. It must be that the gulf between the understanding of a human brain and that of a robot was not so much deep and wide but partook of a difference in kind. In time he would grasp and comprehend. Meanwhile, he must remember that these things were his servants, merely his tools and implements.

He looked into the complicated three-dimensional model and at first his spirit quailed. Through this great whirling wheel light waves and energy waves had been flashing ever since that first unthinkable Beginning when the monobloc had exploded. How could he, with the brain of one man, even the total brain he now wielded, hope ever to thread his way through this mighty maze of stars? A pitiful handful of the constellations had been known and named back on Earth. And even there, what would five millennia have done to the relative motions of the Great Bear, to Orion and to Andromeda?

"And how would you find the Sun we knew as Sol in that maze, Atlas, my friend?" he asked idly watching the unmoving robot. It was the first time he had used the words to any one of these machines and it was curious that his first use of it was to this servile, obsequious worshipper. Was he now beginning to feel like a deity? Was he at last beginning to feel assured of his position in the Cosmos, a god with a court of menials?

"Does the Master wish to return to Earth?" came the metallic reply.

Graeme's ears heard the words and his mind took them in but the significance was seconds before he realized it. Return to Earth! The mere idea had so much brilliance that it blazed in his mind like a supernova. For a moment the vast Galaxy seemed like a smallish friendly pool of warm fires in which Earth swam serenely, merely waiting to be found. Earth! Five millennia in the past he had dwelled there. The sun and the moon, the air and the water, the scents and the shadows. Did he wish to return to Earth? Did he wish to delay his conquest and occupation of all habitable worlds in this galaxy? Yes, by Jupiter, he did. All at once he was consumed with a burning energy to see once more the Earth he remembered. Seen from space, as he had many times seen it, a softly rounded ball of blue and green, turning slowly with its canopy of clouds, the sun gilding one half while the other swam in the darkness that he knew covered the sleep and the revitalization of millions of beings like himself, beings of flesh and blood and bone, of passions and hopes, not mere miracles of engineering like these servants of his.

"I would return to Earth, Atlas," he said clearly and the words were not merely the expression of a sentiment, they were a command, they were the orders of a pilot to his navigator. Atlas turned to go. "The Master will follow?"

It was a vast hall and was positioned behind the outer hull of the ship, beneath the very skin of his metal world. It hummed and crackled with energy and myriads of gleaming lights played over the massive rows of dials and meters. It was a computer and there were many such in the ship, to ensure its smooth and instantaneous response to the controls of the powerhouse that had flamed for five millennia, feeding power into the mechanisms of the ship. It was merely one more computer and Graeme waited.

Atlas walked to a console and his manipulators went out to levers and wheels. The lights ceased to move and the board seemed to be still.

"This, Master," said Atlas, "was to mark the end of our voyage. We were to roam the Galaxy and perform the tasks you Masters had set us. It was known that it would be impossible for us to return through a Galaxy already changing its position with the movements of the Galaxy itself through space, the movements of the stars within it. Therefore, from the start of the voyage co-ordinates were recorded hourly so that in reverse this computer, linked with the ship's telescopes and scanners and astrogation charts can thread our way across the Galaxy back to the Solar System. The Master chose to wake after five millennia. The Masters who sent us out had imposed no limit on our journeyings, no limit except that set by our task. Had we succeeded and had we found Earth-type planets, we would have returned to Earth. We have failed, so far, and so we return to the Master his prerogative to demand of this machine that it shall direct us back to Earth."

In the heady crackling ozonic atmosphere of that great hall Jon Graeme fought for his breath. He stared wolfishly at the silent dials and meters and the still now unwinking lights. Here behind those panels, in those unthinkably numerous circuits and memory banks, lay the secret of the way across the Galaxy back to Earth. Almost did he fall and stumble in the extremity of his emotion. A thousand memories of his past and his youth flooded over him and he felt himself drowning in them, deliciously drowning. It was as though Earth herself lay just outside that hull, an Earth as he remembered it, a kindly sun-warmed, rain-cleansed Earth. By Jupiter, yes, he would go back to Earth but he would go back as a conqueror. Earth should be his base for his Galaxy conquest. Those planets he had stood upon, none of them, close enough maybe to his minimum requirements, none of them would satisfy. Were there an empty planet a counterpart of Earth itself, it would not do. He must have the old-young Earth of his memories. The Earth or nothing.

"It shall not be so," came a thought wave, strong and powerful and his thought leaped across space and met that of Apollo approaching along a corridor. The robot had known through his mind all that was going on in the computer room. Graeme waited, his mind frozen and static, as it had learned to be. No thought passed across his mind; like the computer itself, it was silent and immobile, waiting, waiting . . . "

The robot held a weapon in one of its manipulators. It came into the hall and stood, its glowing eye-sockets turning from the form of Atlas to the still panels of the computer. "It shall not be," it repeated.

Graeme waited and watched, his frozen mind ready. Then his mind lashed out in a swift thrust and immobilized Apollo's weapon. It had been raised against Atlas himself and Graeme was aware of a split in himself. He must save Atlas who was his only link with Earth. In that first thrust into Apollo's mind he had seen all that he had long suspected. Apollo, a machine, had *ambition* to rule the Galaxy, to populate its planets with creatures of his own making, to rule over a vast congeries of worlds on which crawled billions of mindless, soulless automata all obeying the one will of Apollo, the metal god. Graeme burst out laughing and both robots turned, their eye-sockets flashing and staring at him. A thought reached him from Atlas.

"The anger of the god will now be turned on Apollo. The Master will remember that Atlas only exists to serve the Master."

That sickening subservience again, thought Graeme, his mind now working with all the speed and versatility he was now used to. No, by Jupiter, he would *not* destroy Apollo. They were too much alike, were he and this great silent brooding mechanism. They would share many things before it was ended. They would do much together, he and Apollo. But that would come later, of course. Just now, Atlas was his main interest.

It amused him to reach out and grasp the thought patterns of the two robots. They were both now in such a mental state that their mind-barriers seemed to have weakened. He saw in Apollo a sensation akin to human rage that they should return to Earth and leave behind this most promising field of operations, this starfield of rich and potent energies. To Apollo Earth was the place of his manufacture and on Earth he would no longer be a marvel, no longer an emergent metal deity. He would be merely one of many robots. By any means within his power this must be stopped. Graeme felt his thought-pattern reaching into the computer attempting to put it out of action. He chuckled to himself. Apollo was suffering from lack of reason. Destroy Atlas, that was Apollo's best move. Destroy the computer and Atlas could no doubt build another one. He disabled Apollo and satisfied, watched its mind writhe in the cage his brain energy wove round it. It had been a risk. At their first encounter, this thing had negatived his first waking acts and had moved when he had deactivated it. But much had passed since then and the new total mode of Graeme's mind had not stood still. The grip he put upon Apollo's mind was severe enough to show the robot who was master. Once and for all, Apollo must obey. But Graeme knew that he must not destroy this thing. It would prove too valuable to him in the future. Atlas was now his next step. Apollo's turn would come when finally he set foot again on his native earth. He would return a godlike conqueror, he who had crept away a stowaway, an angry resentful fearful stowaway.

His thought turned towards the waiting alert Atlas. What thoughts were passing through that shining brain? There was nothing there but blind, logical worship, the worship of an inferior to a superior, of a creature to a creator. Graeme smiled again and watched the silent Apollo turn and stalk clumsily from the hall, without a word.

Graeme smiled at Atlas. "I am weary of wandering, Atlas, my friend. I will return home for a while. We will set course for Earth. And, Atlas, once again I am impatient. I would see my Earth again as soon as possible. See you to it."

He turned and without a backward glance walked out of the hall. The silence behind him was broken by the resumed humming and crackling of the computer panels. He knew that the lights would be spinning and darting all over that enormous board and that the computer had begun its titanic task of plotting the course for his ship across the trackless starfields.

CHAPTER SEVEN

It was the measure of the enormity of the problem set to it that for many days, the computer, accustomed to solving the most abstruse problems within seconds or minutes, had barely skimmed the surface of this programme after many weeks had passed. Graeme was now in a very fever of impatience. He would step upon Earth *now*, this very moment, if he could, and inwardly he raged at the computer whose operations, which once he had thought so swift, now crawled so slowly through the intricacies of the problem which Atlas had set to it.

Of course, his saner self had some idea of what the machine had been set to do. It had to search through that vast system of millions of stars each hurtling outwards from the centre and each revolving in the complex dance of the Galaxy. It had to find a yellow dwarf star of the G.O. type, of diameter almost 900,000 Earth-miles, of average density 1.41 times that of water, existing by the fusion of naked hydrogen atoms into atoms of helium. Just how many stars of this type in the Galaxy there would be there was of course no knowledge anywhere. The computer must therefore find every star that satisfied all or almost all of the data of Sol. A human brain, a million human brains would take centuries over such a piece of work, even if it were ever possible. The computer had more patience than Jon Graeme would ever have. As the great ship surged backwards and forwards through the whirling starclouds, now at many times the velocity of light, Graeme's spirit quailed at the number of times which the computer completed one inspection and then cleared the board and prepared for the next.

"It is not fast enough for me, Atlas," he told the robot one day as he sat looking into the screens at that hateful and menacing starfield which was all that confronted him. "A new level of investigation is required. Our velocity is not yet fast enough. I am on fire to set foot on Earth, Atlas."

"I have reached the limit of my capabilities, Master," the robot told him. "There is no other way. The computer is the servant of the Master, as Atlas is. It can do no more."

Idly, for a moment, Graeme wondered whether that other, Apollo, the A-type robot, who had evolved emotions so much alike to those of a human would be of any use to him. But he dared not try that. Apollo was so opposed to his returning to Earth that – by Jupiter, that was the solution to the delays of the computer. He turned to Atlas his face blazing.

"Apollo!" he said. "It is responsible for this. I shall bring it here."

Stiffly and silently the robot came and stood before him. The mind-barrier was up and Graeme could not see its thoughts. But he laughed softly to himself. It would be enough that he knew that the barrier was up, always. That way lay the solution.

"The computer must be checked in every part," he told Atlas. "We start afresh. The problem will be solved – must be solved – within twenty earth-hours. This Apollo will remain the prisoner of my mind while the computer works. You will find that there will be a difference."

"It was tampering with it, Master?" came the toneless question. "The work," said Graeme imperiously.

Now the relays chattered faster and faster and the coloured lights ran a dance of fire over the board. Apollo stood immobile while the strength of Graeme's mind held it rigid. It might have been far more simple merely to destroy this thing of metal once and for all. But there was something in Graeme that told him that if he did this, he would live to regret it. Atlas was of use to him on one thing and would be useless to him in another. Besides, his new mode of consciousness gloried in the quite startling fact that a living machine had apparently set itself up in opposition to him, a Man, a Master, the maker of itself.

After four hours. Graeme gave a new command. His brain lashed out to that of Atlas and the other robots who were feeding data into the computer. "Key the power-house to the machine, Atlas. Now it alone will know when we must start to decelerate. I do not think you can have solved the problem of inertia, my friend. I would not wish to flash past my Earth to plunge far past it, so far that return would be as irksome as this journey is."

And so it was. Three hours later, the stars behind them began to blaze out again and the fainter ones began to blaze more brightly. Those ahead dimmed to their normal brilliance and the meters swung round to light-speed, half-light speed, quarter light-speed and so on, down, down, down, into figures that Graeme could comprehend at last.

At a velocity of a mere thousand miles a second, the great ship swept into the Solar System at last. It hurtled past Pluto in the plane of the ecliptic and scythed across the system like a comet. The computer set it in an orbit opposite that of Uranus and for hours it whirled round and round the outer limits of the system as the velocity was gradually reduced. Then Graeme saw Saturn and he wept openly. His mind released that of Apollo from its grip and the robot looked at the computer board, its eye-sockets glowing. Then it turned and walked awkwardly away. Graeme laughed and then wept again. Alternately he laughed and cried as the orbit swept them round through the system, past giant Neptune and greater Jupiter. So to the orbit of Mars and there, at last, there glowed his Earth. The computer banks grew silent as the chattering of the relays died down. The coloured lights slowed and surged desultorily across the panels, winked out one by one and then the whole huge machine was silent, cold and dead, its task completed, its work, the work set to it over five millennia ago, performed.

Avidly, feverishly, Graeme caught his first glimpse of Earth as the ship's orbit swept them past at close to a thousand miles a second. His hands moved out to the controls and he directed Atlas to do likewise.

Round and round in the orbit of Earth they swept many many times before their velocity matched that of the planet. At last Graeme set up an orbit a few thousand miles from the moon and at the same velocity as Earth itself. He took his eyes from the screens and stared round him. The lights began to flicker madly and his senses reeled. He had been awake for over one hundred hours, and labouring under the most powerful emotions. His mind was partly occupied with its grip on the brain of Apollo, and partly on the computer. Outraged nature now took its revenge. The robots turned to watch him. Atlas stood close by him and saw him fall. Like a tree he fell where he had stood and lay there, motionless.

Atlas stared down at him. The god had gone away again. Atlas recalled how it had first seen this Master, lying as it were dead on his couch. Now the god had withdrawn again into that nothingness where he did not speak or move, where that titanic mind was absent. Atlas felt a new emotion rising in it and like many of the other new sensations that had crept into its consciousness since the ship had been at the Centre, it could find no words or ideas in its mind with which to classify and understand it.

Atlas had served and obeyed. It had done the work for which it had been made. The Master had demanded to return to Earth and there Earth was, just as the mind of Atlas remembered it, when it had set forth in this ship over five thousand years before. It was well and it was satisfied. It stopped and lifted up the unconscious body of the god in its metal arms. It strode through the ship and gained the chamber. It laid the god down on the couch and then stood still beside him, not looking down at him but looking instead into this wonderful new mind that had entered its metal. For the first time, maybe, Atlas saw itself for what it was.

* * *

Jon Graeme did not trouble to look into the eyes of Atlas the robot when he woke from that sleep. If he had, it is doubful that he would even have known what he was seeing, nor, even, whether there was anything new to see. For Man, the inveterate and compulsive maker of toys, had always also been an inveterate and compulsive smasher of toys, and he just might have recognized in the eyes of Atlas something that certainly Man had not put there.

Instead, he rose from his couch like a boy with a new and most wonderful career ahead of him, like a man about to step out of prison into a new and marvellous universe. For such it would be and a thousand pictures flooded through his mind of what he would find. When he had left Earth five millennia before he had left a teaming Earth, packed with the technical marvels of many generations, a world where every man had at his behest all the powers of Nature that Science had put into his hand. His nation, the richest and most powerful on Earth, had ruled the globe and there had been peace for over a century, the peace of a strong man armed keeping his camp. And yet, Graeme, himself a Scientist, had been a close witness to the strange sickness that had entered the soul of men via the one single frustration of the Scientist Masters, namely the utter negation of all their plans for exploring and populating Space. The ultimate secrets of matter had been yielded up to Man in his feverish quest. Man was truly the master of his own environment. But that environment was now too small and too narrow; it was a prison revolving in space, a prison to which man was confined, for ever it seemed, by the immense quarantine regulations of the Maker of All. For that is what Man had finally come to recognize that the unthinkable distances in sidereal Space, allied to his own frail, short-lived existence, were the always-unpassable barriers keeping Man from what the Scientist Masters considered to be his true inheritance. Not that Graeme himself had ever considered there was a Maker of all. All he had learned of Science had told him that there had never been a Beginning but that Being had been in existence always. What had irked him always and many like him had been the great probability – now more or less proved by his own travels – that Earth held the sole spark of intelligence at least in his own Galaxy. That being so, had reasoned Graeme and others like him, if Man had not the intelligence and the wit to find a means to surmount those barriers, then his intelligence might as well have never been. And that latter conclusion was one that Graeme's mind, at least, would never even consider.

Well, now he was returning, a god out of the implacable heavens, a god who had ventured near the central fires, who had ranged through the Galaxy and had set foot upon many planets. He was returning with control over powers of his own brain that Man had always possessed but that had always lain unrevealed beneath the blanket of the subconscious. He was returning as a Cosmic King to lead Man out into the garden of the gods, the illimitable universe where every problem would be solved and where there would be no frustration and where at last, Man, the Master of All, would at last be what he had never been before, at peace with himself.

He stared at the globe beneath them and flicked a finger for Atlas.

"Half Earth speed," he snapped and instantly saw the globe beneath him begin to spin lazily. His eyes opened wide in surprise.

"If I was not sure," he muttered to himself, "I would swear it was not Earth."

"It is Earth truly, Master," said Atlas. "But an Earth that even my memory banks do not recall. But five thousand years is a long time, Master, and Man was not a slow mover."

"But – but –" began Graeme as his eyes ran over the details below. "It's not possible. Five thousand years is nothing in the life of a planet. Those mountains, those seas, it isn't possible."

The Rockies had been levelled and the great uplifted

tableland of Tibet and Northern China were rolling hills, covered with what seemed like farms and pasture-land. The Gobi Desert too flourished with trees and foliage. Almost all of North Africa was a great inland sea with only a narrow ridge dividing it from the Mediterranean.

The continents too had altered. In a grotesque and fantastic form they were just recognizable and only just. North and South America were two squat island continents separated from each other by miles of ocean. In the middle of the Pacific was a third large continent, as large as either of the other two. Australia had shrunk or been merged into Asia by a broad land bridge taking in all the South Pacific. A Polar cap swung into view and there was no Pole. At least there was no ice-cap, no miles-thick cap of eternal ice. Instead, and Graeme could now scarcely believe his eyes – instead, there was a green land at this Antarctic Pole, a greenland with at its centre a round black cap. He sat down on the one seat he had provided for himself in the control room with Atlas looming above him and Apollo, now returned quietly, on the other. This was his Earth, this new and strange planet in which already he felt himself a stranger. For the new mind he now used was telling him of the myriad implications he must read out of even what little he had already seen.

He speeded the ship up and it flashed round the world halting every now and again while he stared silently at the screens. At the northern Pole was another of the strange black caps and it was set in the midst of what looked like a warm tropical sea. He went down and the ship hovered over cities. They were gigantic, immense cities, cities such as back in the Twenty-Third Century they had never even dreamed of. There were cities that seemed to engulf continents; cities built as it were in the middle of seas; cities built where once snow-clad mountains had reared their impregnable peaks. And there was traffic. There were hosts of small fliers, darting like butterflies close to the ground and there were great globe-ships crossing the seas. None came up to investigate their coming and there came no signals through their screens or radio. It was as though the strange globe had not seen them or if so, was evincing no interest. Jon Graeme's eyes gleamed and his jaw was set.

"We will land," he snapped to both the robots and instantly into his mind flashed a warning from Apollo, a warning in a very different tone from any with which he had ever before addressed him.

"It is not wise, Master," said Apollo's mind. "Earth is no longer the world we left. We will not be at home there. It is strange and foreign and hostile. We will go back to the stars, the friendly, remote stars where fire is Master, and all Being is in conflict."

"Master," said the mind of Atlas. "You are right. You must land. It is so far and it has been so long. Apollo, you speak evil in what you say. There is the birthplace of us all. We ourselves were forged on that Earth and down there dwell the descendants of the very Masters who lovingly fabricated us. Even the Master himself was born there, even he was called into being there. But he was created and not like us, made."

"So Atlas no longer worships the Man," said Apollo's mind and Graeme knew that, for a moment, they were ignoring him, but were carrying on some argument they had doubtless indulged in while he had slept the long sleep of five thousand years. He listened silently.

"Atlas still worships Man," came Atlas's reply. "But the worship is offered because he is Man and not because he is a god. The term god it appears to me is but a relative term. Your mismade monsters no doubt worship you as a god. I worship Graeme because he is a Man."

Jon Graeme laughed quietly within himself. Well, his deity had been shortlived, after all. As well so, deity might have proved a most uncomfortable cloak. And anyway, he thought wryly, how could you ever possibly hope to deceive a machine?

"We go down," he said and got to his feet. The ship was now orbiting slowly enough that he could ease her down on the anti-gravity beams with manual control.

Rather of set purpose, he had paid little attention to the part of the globe where he had originated, Northern Europe. He stared down now and recognized the shape, enormously altered. Britain was a mere bulge at the top of North Europe and the joined landmass of Scandinavia lunged at the spot where once the English Channel flowed. Slowly and easily he brought the ship down on her many stilts of anti-gravitic energy in a spot which could only have been central England in the old days.

Like pillars of rock the beams held and then as his fingers touched controls they truncated until they vanished completely and the ship lay in a hollow made by her own weight, in the centre of England. Five thousand years before she had hurtled up to the stars a brave new task force to conquer the Cosmos. Now she returned, after many billions of miles and with many scars, to the Earth that had made her.

It was night outside and the land seemed to be deserted. There were many tall dark shapes which Graeme's hungry soul told him could only be trees. There was the sound of water running not far away and his heart yearned for the outside. He caused the great door to be opened and the great cartridge revolved in its socket and yawned inwards. He stood at the portal breathing in the warm heady night air and his spirit bounded within him, bounded as it had never done before. He, Jon Graeme, had done the forbidden thing, he had been to the far stars and had lived and seen and had returned with tales to tell such as no returned travellers had ever had to tell since Time began.

Ladders were run out and he ran down until his feet stood upon the soil. The very touch set a thrill through his every tissue. The two robots followed and they stood staring silently round them. They unlike him, could see as well in the dark as by day and the night was not dark to them. Atlas's mind touched his. "Master, they are coming."

"Who?" jerked Graeme's mind and for an instant a streak of fear ran in him.

"Your people come, Master," said Atlas.

An intense thrill ran through him at the thought. These would be the descendants of his own people whom he had left behind. Tears were blinding his eyes as he looked from side to side to see who it was that might be coming.

There was only one small flyer and it came in from the south like a gleaming dragonfly and landed on the turf not ten yards from where he stood. Like a feather it landed and Graeme was prepared to swear that not a blade of grass would have been disturbed. In his time they had not had such craft, even with the anti-gravity beams. Well, five thousand years was a very long time.

He heard laughing voices and recognized the voices of women amongst them. It electrified him into a purely instinctive and totemic shame that he was naked. He had not bothered aboard the ship to fabricate garments for himself but it should have been his first thought on preparing to land on Earth. Also, there was the climate. Why did he not feel cold in the night of northern England? In the darkness a dull flush covered his face as the laughing voices grew nearer.

There were four, two men and two women. The lights from the flyer lit up their tall, young figures, lightly clad in tunics. Without speaking one of them came up and held out a small bundle to Graeme. "You will not really need this, Jon Graeme, but we wear them for harmony and for colour. We welcome you home after your long voyage."

Stupefied, Graeme took the light silk-like tunic and slipped it on. The voice was speaking to him in English, or, was it? Certainly, the sense of the words came to his brain as English. Telepathy, of course? But no. His questioning brain found no holding place in the brain of the man before him, not even could he find any evidence of a mind-screen. The face of the man was smiling and bland and revealed nothing of the thoughts behind the fair flowing hair.

"You know who I am," Graeme spoke the words aloud and the other laughed. "Of course we know all about you," he replied. "Marta, Hans, Seena come here and look at the hero we learned about in our history books at school."

The four gathered round him smiling and talking all at once. His mind became confused and strangely, almost at once, the talking ceased. He felt confused and strange. He should be striding masterfully into this world like a King and a Conqueror. Instead he was being treated as a legendary hero of the olden times, by this group of laughing youngsters.

"We have come to take you to our village," said the first young man. "I am Kyril and it is my duty and pleasure to receive you. Your coming was noticed and recognized. I might say that your arrival has settled a two thousand year old controversy. Many thought you did not exist and that the whole story of your flight in the robot ship was a fairy-story left by those old people of the dark times. I always believed it myself but then I am a romantic. But we do not need to talk out here. Come, there is room in our flyer."

"I cannot come just like this," stammered Graeme looking to each side towards Apollo and Atlas, standing still beside him. Kyril looked at them thoughtfully. "Ah, yes, I had forgotten them," he said absently. He turned towards the other man and nodded. "Would you see to it, Hans?" Then he turned towards Graeme, "It is arranged. Tell your – er – robots to go back to the ship and then you will come with us."

There was nothing else that Graeme could do. He gave the orders to his lieutenants and they turned and went back to the ship. The door closed and the great ship rested there, a blacker globe in the darkness, just as she had plunged through the starfields during his five millennial flight. A small shiver ran through him at the thought of leaving what had been his only world for so long a time, a feeling, he wondered, akin to the fear of the new-born to emerge from the womb. An odd simile.

Like a feather the craft rose and shot straight up for a mile and then levelled out and sped across the sleeping land. Graeme looked at his companions. The two men looked young and strong and very handsome. The women were beautiful, so beautiful that it almost hurt his eyes to look at them. He had been absent from women for so long that their actuality hit him like a blow and dazed him. His scientific mind had never, in his far-distant youth, interested itself in them and now the accumulation of thousands of years of repression, resulted in this new and unwelcome intoxication.

"Where are you taking me?" he asked and he hoped fervently that they would not detect the nervousness in his voice. "To your capital city?"

"Oh no," said the other. "We don't have those things now, you know. We're taking you home. Our mission is to, well, rehabilitate you, reorientate you on your homecoming after so long an absence."

"Is that considered necessary?" asked Graeme stiffly and Kyril nodded his head gravely.

"Oh, very necessary, indeed," he said. "Please don't think me patronizing but five thousand years *is* a very long while and you have been – er – asleep during most of that time – "

"Now, look," said Graeme argumentatively, "that couldn't have been in the legend. No one on earth could have known how many centuries the meters were set for – " He paused as a newer and still stranger thought came to him. "Another thing. I went aboard the ship in secrecy. No one knew I was there, I am positive of that. How has this legend grown at all? The ship was crewed entirely by robots. There was no air in her except what I made with the apparatus I used. No one on Earth knew where I had gone so how can you have been expecting me?"

"You see," laughed Kyril gently. "There is much to be told. Have patience, Jon, you will learn everything and you will be happy when you know what five thousand years has done for the world and for the men of Earth, those men you loved so much that you risked your life to ensure that one man, at least, should see the stars."

"Yes," replied Graeme slowly, his mind confused between pleasure at hearing his own name spoken by human lips for the first time for so long, and puzzlement at the problems surrounding him. "Yes, I have solved the problem we found so great back there. I have ranged through the entire Galaxy and stood upon many planets. I have been close to the Hub of the galaxy where are flame and primeval fragments of that titanic explosion which marked the birth of our universe. I have – "

"That accounts for the faint penumbra we noticed," Kyril said Hans and all four of them looked at him gravely but without speaking. He smiled to himself. They were beginning to notice things.

"Yes," he said proudly. "No man of our race has been closer to the Centre, no man of our race has stood upon so many worlds. I bring back to Earth many secrets, many new facets of knowledge, many things that have lain hidden in my subconscious mind until the energies of the Centre unlocked the door – "

"We have arrived, Jon," said Kyril dryly and the flyer dropped lightly to the earth. Graeme smiled to himself. These young people might smile on the other side of their faces before so very long.

The "village" was small and appeared to be built of illuminated ice-blocks. At least that was his first impression as he climbed down with the others. The dwellings of many shapes and sizes, dotted the terrain with no thought for order and regimentation. Most were illuminated but in some, here and there, the lights were going out. Kyril led the way to a large house upon a hill. It was brilliantly lighted in every colour of the spectrum and there were many blank places where no colour or light came through to his retina at all. For a second he frowned at this. At the edge of his consciousness clamoured the explanation but his mind was too stubborn to receive it yet.

It was warm within, pleasantly warm and dry and a fountain played in the centre courtyard round which were curtained rooms. It reminded him somewhat of the atrium of a Roman villa remembered from his youth. Or Greece, yes, there were many suggestions of Ancient Greece about this house. They even reclined on couches as at the symposia, as he found when the meal was served.

He found that these people ate fruit and cereals of many kinds, some familiar and some, as was to be expected, new and strange. But in front of himself, he found beakers of the liquid food upon which he had subsisted since his awakening. This now did need some explanation. They could have reasoned that after five thousand years of suspended animation in the nutrient fluid and then life on a liquid diet necessary for a creature whose digestive organs had been inactive for so long, it could not be a solid diet. But this, he tasted, this was an exact copy of what nourishment he had been using since he awakened. He opened his mouth to speak, then saw that Kyril was standing up.

"In your day, Jon," he said, "you had a custom of drinking toasts. As a student of antiquity I know many of your old customs. I call now for a toast to the marvel of your return." There was a little titter from one of the girls and he frowned at her. Graeme too looked serious and wondered if his attitude might seem pompous. Anyway, his return was marvellous enough in all conscience. His eyes caught the eyes of the other girl, she named Marta, and there was no frivolity there. Only a glow of friendship and a hint of yet another emotion, an emotion he could almost think of as pity.

"Even in this marvellous age," went on Kyril, "the return of an elder brother from a journey of five thousand years is a marvel. Jon, we welcome you back to your family, the family of Mankind, and to a reawakening to a new birth such as I think even you never looked forward to."

He drank from his beaker and Jon Graeme did likewise. He was looking into those dark eyes of Marta and trying to formulate in his mind some idea of the unknown colour that lurked in their depths.

There came a titanic rumble from without and they all came to their feet. Kyril looked at Hans. "They are attempting to escape," he rapped out. "As we thought. What was the power? Is it possible?"

Hans laughed confidently. "Quite impossible, Kyril. Over a hundred times was the increase. Might as well try to move an asteroid. We know all about them. They'll still be there. There'll be some destruction though. They've got some strong stuff in there."

A strange suspicion was forming in Graeme's mind. "What was that?" he demanded of Kyril. "There's something in my mind – " He staggered where he stood as a tremendous call came to his mind and it could come from only one source, from Atlas. Atlas was in trouble. Then it was blanked out, quietly and efficiently and effortlessly blanked out. By Apollo's mind? No, that familiar echo was absent. He seized Kyril's arm. "If any damage comes to my ship," he began fiercely and his hand reached for his weapon, the weapon, alas, that remained on board his ship. He found himself facing them all four and they were regarding him silently. They did not speak nor did their minds speak. For an odd and hideous moment he had the feeling that they were four judges surveying a condemned man.

"It is your robots," said Kyril tonelessly. "They have tried to take the ship up. We have prevented them, that is all."

CHAPTER EIGHT

THERE was something hideously wrong here, thought Graeme to himself. This was not the way he had intended to mark his triumphant return to the Earth. There were undercurrents here that he could not understand, nor could he make any contacts with the minds behind those four serious faces.

"And what right have you to interfere with my ship?" he began to bluster. "It seems that I am wasting my time here, with you children. Take me at once to someone in authority, your King, President, Prime Minister, whatever the office. I bring stores of knowledge that will be of inestimable value to Earth."

It was Kyril who spoke. "There must be apologies, Jon Graeme, of that there is no doubt. We were too abrupt but the danger was one that perhaps you would not understand. Did you but know the history of the Earth through the past few thousand years you might forgive our precipitate action. Your robots were the first that have been since in this world for over a thousand years. Because they were with you, and were obviously under your command, we let them go back to the starship, alone. But your robots are no longer mere robots. You will know of this, of course?"

"They have evolved," replied Graeme impatiently. "If human protoplasm can evolve, so it seems, can metal evolve until it can think. Both the protoplasm and the metal are of the same basic elements. I see nothing strange in that. My lieutenants are my servants. They obey me in my every command. What have you done to them?"

"Nothing, as yet," replied Kyril. "So your theory is that they have evolved into something more than machines. It is logical, anyhow. Our forefathers knew more than we thought. Their foresight was indeed the foresight of prophecy. Your ship is safe, Jon, and your crew is immobile, waiting, as all good metal should wait, the hand of the craftsman. It alters my plans. We will return there. We cannot stay here, in any case. Come, we will go now."

For a moment, Jon Graeme, nettled enough already, was about to protest when it came home to him with full force that he would be in a far better position near his ship than here in this strange village of these latterday Earthmen who seemed as alien to him as any fancied denizen of a distant world. In the ship lay all his power, his weapons, his machines, his servants. He allowed himself to be escorted back to the flyer. The village now seemed to be all in darkness and they saw no one.

The flyer hovered a moment over the now-empty house and Kyril played with the studs of a board set in the wall. Graeme's eyes bulged as he looked down and saw the house disintegrate before his eyes. The slabs and plinths of crystal seemed to flow into each other so that they became an amorphous, inchoate mass. This glowed for a while and then the darkness covered the spot where the house had been. Speechless, he looked at Kyril but the young man had turned away from the board and was standing staring ahead of him. Graeme could find no words with which to express himself.

The scene was exactly as they had left it so short a while ago. The ship loomed up a deeper black than its surroundings. Or at least, so Jon Graeme thought at first. Then he noted that where before its vast weight had depressed the earth by perhaps one-eighth of its diameter, now the depression seemed to be about one-quarter. The ship was evidently settling still more into the earth. He longed to get back on board of her and to surround himself with his familiar surroundings. But the flyer did not land immediately.

Again at the board, Kyril handled the studs and levers. Below where they were grew a house, an ethereal house of crystal and diamond, an unreal fairy house of pillars and plinths, of every conceivable geometrical pattern and of many that were not in any geometry known to Graeme. This was black magic. There was no other word for it than that. He reached for Kyril's arm, frowned as he saw the young man recoil from his touch as from the touch of a leper. Hot words sprang to his lips and died when Kyril conquering the feeling he had betrayed, came close to him and put an arm round his shoulder.

"Don't be puzzled, Jon," the young man said gently. "You know, five millennia is a very long while. Science and technology have not stood still since you left. That is one of our more primitive methods of housebuilding. It may seem like magic to you but is a mere matter of manipulating the basic materials that are always round us. As you have said, all material things are constructed from the same basic atoms."

Graeme laughed a little nervously. "Of course," he said huskily. "I shall look forward to seeing many marvels, no doubt. I think perhaps that I too will be able to reveal many of my own."

"Your very presence here with us tonight," said Kyril gaily, "is the greatest marvel of all. There is not a man or woman on Earth who does not tonight envy us the privilege of being with you here."

"No need to overdo it, Kyril," said Hans with a twisted mouth. Seena looked mournful but on the face of Marta was a wonderful placidity.

"The dwelling is a replica of the other one," said Kyril as he led the way into the house, now illuminated and casting a circular glow all round it, a glow which washed over the hull of the starship, so close were they. ""I thought it best not to confuse you with too many marvels at once."

"We might talk better aboard my ship," said Graeme, attempting to be friendly. It was difficult with this youth whose every look and spoken word seemed to hold unseen nuances. To put it bluntly, he told himself he was feeling very uncomfortable with these young people dressed as they were for a Greek drama and in surroundings something akin to what the slopes of Olympus must have been.

"We thank you," said Kyril. "It will be our pleasure later on. Until dawn I think it best that we rest and refresh ourselves in this house. It will be a novelty to you, Jon, to sleep once more in a house?"

Graeme laughed. Novelty was far too mild a word to use.

The dawn was breaking over the trees as they reclined again and now that he was once more close to his ship, Graeme began to relax. After all, these people were doubtless merely messengers, sent to familiarize him with the new environment he must learn to know. At least, they were pleasant. presentable youngsters enough. No doubt, many preparations would be going on in the cities. His arrival would be celebrated with great acclaim. He would travel from city to city, showing himself to the people, as the Star-Conqueror, the one frail human who had spanned the vastness of the Galaxy and had returned to tell of its wonders. Kyril's first words shattered his mood of self-complacency.

"You asked to be taken to our capital city, Jon," he said. "We have no capital city but there *are* cities and these you will see, in good time. But you will meet no Kings, No Presidents, no Prime Ministers. We do not harbour such anachronisms nor do we afford the luxury of Governments."

If this was true, thought Graeme, how oddly had humanity evolved politically? The fellow was talking of some Utopia where government was not necessary. It had been theorized centuries before his own birth and had been blown helter-skelter like the immaterial froth it had been.

"In your mind," went on Kyril calmly, "you class us as children. Perhaps to you, born over five millennia ago, we may seem to be so. But – " He paused and his eyes gleamed. He leaned forward on his couch. "I, Kyril, Jon Graeme," he went on, "came to receive you on your return as the leading citizen of this section of the globe. For sentimental reasons we preserve the ethnic names of our world and this is the North European Sector. I am – or rather I was – its chief citizen, the nearest equivalent to the King or President you spoke of."

"A Utopia of children," chuckled Graeme and in his mind was exultation at the ease with which the subjugation of such a race could be accomplished.

It was a new voice that answered him and he turned towards the girl Marta. She had not spoken before and her voice in his ears was pure music. It soothed and lulled him but it did not soften the harsh shock he received from her next words.

"Unwittingly, Jon Graeme," she said, "you use a word that is perhaps our only magic word – children. It is the price we have paid for everything else, that we deny ourselves the right to bear them. For future generations this hardship will not be. We of this generation must suffer the loss."

"You mean – you can't have children," ejaculated Graeme. Some great natural disaster perhaps, some decay of the germ-plasm. That would be the end of the species. He stared at her dumbly.

"In a world such as we have made, Jon," she said, "there is room for but few young ones. We limit ourselves severely. We are as fruitful as any species but we have set a limit. You think of us as careless children Jon, but Kyril there has lived seven hundred years, while Hans and Seena have lived five hundred. To you we may seem to be infants but in our world we are mature middle-aged persons."

Jon Graeme's ears could almost hear the vibration of the force waves that held that immaterial house in being as he digested the implications of her words. That they were true, strangely enough, he had no slightest doubt. These people did not need to lie to him. If what she said then was true she too was centuries old – he did not care to pursue that subject, as he stared at her smooth cheeks and glowing eyes. He laughed shakily.

"So the research into longevity was successful," he said eagerly. "Mankind has conquered old age and the decay of the tissue. Now, at last we will be able to go to the stars. With my starship and many like it we will go through the Galaxy, maybe out to the further galaxies. I have found the secret of exceeding the speed of light. I have sped through the starfields at many times the speed of light. Oh, we will do wonders when I meet your Scientists. This is indeed a new birth for mankind. With your immortality and my velocity-drive, we will truly be masters of the Galaxy."

"Quite useless, Kyril," spoke up Hans impatiently. "You can see how it is. We but waste our time. When the project was first launched it was my first thought that here comes the speck of dust that will grind the machine to a halt. Do it now, as the surgeon does at the first sign. You can see the tendencies behind the words. This is all old stuff, dead and forgotten many centuries ago. We waste our time."

"We have no time to waste, Hans," came Kyril's reply, slowly and as though he weighed every word. "Our time has run out and we have but the one last duty to perform."

Graeme could catch no understanding of what they were talking about and anyway he was losing interest. In their speech together these people left gaps between their words and it was obvious that there were many concepts and idioms in their talk together that were meaningless to him. It did not matter much. Time would solve those things. Let him now get back to his ship and start things going. He rose and went to a wall. He watched the sun come up over that forest and he marvelled at the immense acreage of the timber. He turned enthusiastically towards Kyril.

"This was England when I left Earth," he said. "It was the land of my birth. You say it is now a part of North Europe. What of the other nations, the French, the Americans, the Russians. How is the political atmosphere of Earth these days? No doubt there will be a World

Government with a Council of Ministers, controlling the armed forces. Tell me everything. You treat me like a child. I don't altogether know whether to believe the tale told me by your charming Marta but, even so, let me remind you that I myself am over five thousand years old and I don't suppose there's anyone of Earth able to cap that."

He meant his words as a joke but Hans stared at him as though he had uttered an obscenity while the two girls shifted their shoulders a little. Only Kyril smiled faintly.

"You are our elder brother," he said frankly, "and we will be open with you. As soon as your sphere was detected; it was before you even entered the Solar System, we knew all about you. We knew who you were, where you had been, what your condition was, in fact everything. When you decided to land in my Sector, it fell as my duty to receive you. My companions elected to be with me and so they have fallen into the trap into which my position forced me. You will forgive them if they sometimes show a little anger. It was the one thing we overlooked."

Graeme looked from one to the other. Why did these ancient children speak in unintelligible riddles? "All right," he granted. "We'll take it from there. You may know all about me. Your rapport certainly seems to excel anything we've developed in the ship. Now it's my turn. I want to know everything about this Earth of mine. I have plans for this Earth and I must know all about it before I can make my plans."

Kyril's level eyes surveyed him and there was now a broad smile on the face. It almost amounted to a chuckle and it was taken up by the two girls and left only Hans sulking. But it was not an offensive laugh and Graeme himself joined.

"The history of five thousand years to be compressed in an hour at dawn," said Kyril. "Five millennia! You know it isn't possible, Jon."

"But I *must* know it all, Kyril," said Graeme enthusiastically. "I will lead Mankind out to the stars. We will populate the Galaxy. I know many planets that would tolerate enough alteration to their ecology to make them fit for mankind. But I must know my Earth before I can lead Man to the stars."

"You are too late, Jon Graeme," smiled Kyril. "Man has no need to go to the stars. The stars have come down to us."

"The stars came down," repeated Graeme stupidly. The sense of the words took some time getting to him. If they were literally true then – but of course they were not true. He knew; he had been to the stars.

"Your words are a simile, of course," he replied politely. "Unable himself to rationalize the fact staring him in the face that man would never go to the stars, over the centuries Man has lulled his restless spirit with some – " He realized himself as he was speaking that his words were not making any sense. A hot flush of anger spread over his face as he saw the look of disgust come into the face of Hans.

"You mean," he rambled on, "that while I have been star-roving, people from the stars have visited Earth? It was indeed speculated upon in many of our legends and stories. Tell me all about it, these people from the stars. Are they like we are? Does their intelligence match ours? What puzzles me is that in my wanderings I must have covered just about every quarter of the Galaxy and stood upon many planets that might support life in some form. Not once did I encounter intelligence."

"Our visitors were not from our Galaxy," said Kyril calmly. "And they were not *people*."

Now this, said Graeme to himself, is pure fantasy. These young people were making game of him. Not from our Galaxy indeed. Then from which "Stars" had they come. He laughed pleasantly at Kyril.

"I think that maybe it is you who need sleep, Kyril," he said. "Always you talk to me in riddles as though I was a child. Well, in my age, in all ages, the young were accustomed to speak thus to their elders. That is a matter we can go into some other time. Now, I have things to see and to plan."

"You don't believe me, then?" asked Kyril frowning in puzzlement.

"Did I say so?" came back Graeme smiling. "Let's leave the whole thing, shall we. You know, I'm beginning to think that the basis of all the differences between you people and myself is mainly a question of semantics. We just aren't communicating. Now, I would suggest that we stay close to the actual, the tangible and seeable. The airy metaphysics we'll leave until such time as I have been able to get a mental view of this world and what it is like now."

Kyril looked at him from brooding eyes and then glanced at his three companions. They nodded and he rose with a light laugh.

"The practical technological scientist of the Twenty-Third Century wins this round," he said. "We will go and you will see this world. When you have seen it then you will want to sleep, I promise you that."

"The cities, the people, the engineering shops, the laboratories," said Graeme with a boyish eagerness. "All these I want to see and more. I am hungry for the marvels that fifty centuries will have dragged out of reluctant Mother Nature. As a young man, those ages past, I speculated many, many times. I am on fire to see which of my idle dreams have been fulfilled."

"Then you have come home to a world beyond even your best anticipations," said Kyril. "In this world now it is difficult to imagine any dream of man which has gone unfulfilled."

Graeme felt again a touch of irritation. Why did they have to talk such nonsense? Well, he had eyes and ears and a superb intellect. He would look and hear and study. He would learn more than they could ever tell him.

"We will go to the cities first," said Marta and she took Graeme by the arm and led him outside to the flyer. The touch of her fingers was very soft. He gave a glance towards his black starship, now greying in the dawn. Soon, he would be back on board to make his plans.

A city lay beneath the hovering flyer and now that they were but a mile or less above its pinnacles, Graeme's mind rocked slightly as he looked down. This was truly a city of fantasy. Never in all of their wildest dreams back there had they envisaged anything quite like this.

How many miles in diameter it was he could not estimate. It was white, it was coloured and yet there were blanks where no colour registered on his retina. Now at last he was forced to the dismaying conclusion that there were colours beyond either the violet or the red which these latter-day people saw but which his eyes could not see. That evolution could go so far in a matter like this staggered him.

The size of the city set his mind reeling. Immense as it was it gave the impression of ethereality but as the flyer settled slowly down between the towers and pinnacles brightly lit by the sun, he began to realize that all his comparisons of size and magnificence must be forgotten. When the flyer touched ground and getting out he looked up, it was as though those pinnacles almost touched the clouds. He turned to Marta. "This is – " he hesitated, " – this is a wonderful place."

There were many fountains playing and birds singing in the air. He saw animals stalking backwards and forwards and for a moment quailed when he saw a hot yellow tiger staring at him boldly. Kyril smiled.

"They will not harm you, Graeme," he said. "There are no more wild beasts on Earth. We let them roam at will in our cities. There is always food for them. Here you will at last see the lion lying down with the lamb."

Graeme felt bemused. "But the people who live here: there must be many millions of them to inhabit such a city. Where are they: I can see none or hear them?"

"They come back occasionally," Kyril said casually. "Into all our lives comes once again the spirit of change.

We would go back to our childhood and the things that were important to us then. You see these walls, Jon, they are not the ethereal gossamer of the house we built for you. These are solid and actual. You will find much marble here and crystal. There is gold and platinum and many a metal which you in your day did not know of. They are hard and real and actual. As I said, sometimes our young minds grow a little weary and we creep back here to some such place to see again the marvels we once wrought from natural elements and once thought lovely and enduring. It usually cures us for, you know, there is no endurance in material. All must dwindle and perish and die. This city here, for instance. We built it and set its automatic machinery in motion, over five hundred years ago. It would endure for five thousand more with scarcely a change unless a party of us should suffer the urge to unmake it and remake it in a different mode."

"Again you are talking over my head," snapped Graeme impatiently. "Little of what you say is comprehensible to me. Let me meet the people of the city and I will talk to them. People who built a marvel such as this will be towering masters of technology and I would learn from them."

"There are no people in this city, Jon," said Kyril and Graeme stood still and looked at him. Then he looked round him at the towers and the pavilions and the pinnacles, at the birds and at the tame sleek beasts padding round them sniffing curiously.

"No people!" he repeated stupidly and his shoulders drooped. If there were no people in such a city as this was, where could he begin with his plans?

"No people, Jon," said Kyril gently. "Marta, perhaps you should tell him. Perhaps he will believe you where he distrusts me."

Marta took hold of Graeme's hand. "Scattered all over the globe, Jon, there are hundreds of cities such as this, some like this and others in different styles. You might perhaps find one built like a city of your era. It depends upon which school of thought or love of which antiquity ruled the builders at the time. But the people who built them have grown up, Jon, they have moved on, such things no longer interest them. They are like the toys of one's childhood, dear remembered things to be picked up later and dreamed over and then laid aside again for the *real* things of life. You might even find a city here and there still inhabited – we would not know. In time that city too will be abandoned. You see, it is perishable, it must crumble and die. And such things cannot long interest a true human being."

He stared uneasily. The last three words had seemed to hold some special significance. During the last few years of his star-roving, as he had become more and more conscious of the limitless powers of his total brain, he had imagined that he was growing into a true complete human being, no longer crippled by frustrations and dichotomies. He did not dare to bring up that subject now but just looked at her beautiful face and decided that she was at least telling him truth, at least such truth as she knew. If a city such as this, and many like it, had ceased to interest its builders, then prodigal indeed must be the resources of the world. He would find plenty to do here when his plans were made.

"Round two goes to you, Kyril," he laughed to the man and the girl. "If you wanted to stun me, you've succeeded. Now you have set me on fire to meet your marvellous people, your scientists and chemists, your mathematicians and engineers. When can I meet them? I could almost worship at the feet of men of such calibre as would call this city an expendable toy."

"Meeting them would be difficult, Jon," replied Kyril and Graeme was convinced there was a hint of evasion in his tones. "We dwell now not in great congregations but in small groups, even often quite alone. We can make our homes in any part of the globe we desire. Climate has been tamed and all the Earth is habitable."

"But you must have a *Government* of some sort," protested Graeme. "What you picture is sheer anarchy, with each man doing just what he fancies. Only chaos could be the result of that. There must be some sort of – " his words laboured and he remembered the faint smiles on the faces of the three and the animosity on the face of Hans. He had been going to say Council but the word seemed tame and insufficient. A council that could rule a world of such proportions would truly be a group of supermen. "Where are your treasuries, your shipyards, where do you build your flyers and make your food and your clothing? How is business and commerce carried on between you. I saw continents still separate on the globe. There must be communication between them."

"It's going to be harder than even we thought," said Kyril with a laugh. "You must believe me, Jon, we have none of such things in the world. Their usefulness has passed and we no longer need them. All the material things we need we make for ourselves on the spot by manipulation of the atoms, as you have seen. What we cannot do in that way, is manufactured for us by automatic machinery keyed in to our minds so that we have what we want almost as soon as our minds frame the desire."

A point of contact at last. "Robots," said Graeme enthusiastically. "Of course that's it, I see it now. As we foretold Man lives now in a paradise of plenty, served by a myriad of robots who are his immortal slaves – "

Kyril's face had grown hard all in an instant. Indeed, there was a curious silence descending on all four of his guides. Seena looked at him intently from between long lashes and on Marta's face was again a look of sadness. The face of Hans held only greater contempt and hostility.

"There is not a robot existing in this Earth, Jon Graeme," said Kyril steadily. "They were destroyed in the Great War of two thousand years ago. The robots you have brought back in your ship are the only ones of the breed now existing."

But Graeme missed the significance of the words in

his new exultation. They had no robots, no governments, no armies, navies, no starships, no cities or centres of civilization. While he held all the trump cards, he would just step in and take over. He laughed airily.

"If you have no central government, no rulers," he went on. "How was your Great War carried on and who gave the orders for the wanton destruction of your robots? I'd say whoever it was was a crank and no true scientist. Who gave those orders?"

"The Monitors told us what to do," said Kyril and now at last even Graeme was conscious of a strange electric tingle in the charged air that surrounded them.

CHAPTER NINE

"The Monitors," repeated Graeme and there was a broad smile on his face. "A fanciful term. And who are the Monitors, might one ask? Your rulers, I should imagine, your wise men and elders? Where do they live? I will go to them and talk with them. It seems to me that for some quaint reason I am not to meet the people of my world. You four are the only humans so far that I have seen. You tell me the wonderful cities are empty. I'll tell you, Kyril, my friend, I am getting very tired of all this. Just what I expected when I returned from my star-wanderings would be hard to say but it was certainly not this. You welcomed me on my arrival; this is scarcely *my* notion of a welcome."

"It is so difficult," sighed Kyril with a wry smile. "You know, Jon, you and I are almost aliens, each to the other. There are so few points of contact. You yourself say that in our communications together there are large gaps which do not come through to your consciousness. The semantic barrier is very strong, we have so few common areas of reference."

"I don't think that matters so much," said Graeme frankly. "It seems very obvious to me that we are not going to cooperate. Your views of life are so vastly different from mine that they will never meet. It seems to me – but, first things first, these Monitors, who and what are they, and where are they to be found?"

"I told you," said Kyril patiently. "They came to Earth two thousand years ago. They do not come from our own Galaxy, they come from a star-system in a galaxy so distant from us that the whole island universe appears as a mere faint smudge of light in our most powerful telescopes, even those set up on the Moon and on Pluto. They are – no, there is no use of describing them to you, there are no holding places in your mind to accept the concepts."

Graeme kept still. The fantasy again. But he was a man of hard common sense and he would weigh the evidence. If what Kyril was saying was literal truth then there was some way in which he could understand it. Maybe he was wasting chances in scoffing at these youngsters. Mere age meant nothing, after all.

"A distant galaxy," he mused. "Now that means a mode of passage quite outside of any material things we know or can even imagine. The distant galaxies are uncountable millions of light-years away. How do they reach us here? What sort of ships have they? What do they look like?"

"They have no ships," said Kyril frankly. "They need no ships. They tell us that once, long, long ages ago they needed ships in which to navigate the cosmos. They have outgrown this need."

"Outgrown it." Graeme repeated bemused. "Then they do not breathe nor do they feel cold or heat. They have no bodies, in other words?" His lips was curling slightly. He felt, somehow, that he knew what was coming. But he was wrong.

Kyril laughed. "No, not what you are thinking, Jon. They are not spirits or angels or supernatural beings from the old religious myths. They have bodies, perhaps rather I should say organisms. They can adapt and rearrange these organisms to suit their environment. Indeed, their whole philosophy and mode of being is quite outside our understanding even after two thousand years. But we are learning something new every century. We have long life and we do not end in a few short years. They gave us little actually when they came, merely the philosophy and the evidence of our senses that it works. The rest we must do for ourselves. They left us, when they went away, the Monitors. In the largest sense the Monitors are our rulers."

"But the Monitors, I thought, *were* the people, the beings, from beyond the galaxy?" put in Graeme.

"Just our slipshod way of putting things," laughed Kyril. "You see, they themselves have no real name, in our tongue. We termed them the Monitors for want of anything better. They have names for themselves, of course, but they do not mean anything to us. The Monitors we really meant were the polar axis powerhouses."

"I saw them," ejaculated Graeme. "What are they?"

"Oh," said Kyril casually. "They are immense powerhouses and a mass of thinking machines. From a climatic and sidereal point of view they monitor the life of this planet. They can alter the axis of the globe and they can change its tilt in the plane of the ecliptic. They rearrange our climates and they supervise our food-growing – "

"Like a nurse-maid," laughed Graeme and Marta smiled.

"Just like a nurse-maid, Jon," she said. "Without them we would be savages at the mercy of wind and tempest and plague, fighting every step of our way against the elements and the circumstances of being. We would be just as men were thousands of years ago. Just as you – "

"Just as I am now, eh?" put in Graeme grimly. "Oh, I know you have me down as a primitive savage come out of the barbaric past. Let me tell you, those were no days of hardship. They were glorious days, days of heroism and adventure. Men pitted their little strength against a hostile nature. Some won and some lost. It seems to me that this is the essence of life and not the mere bending to the will of some weird creatures from somewhere indefinite who seem to know what is best for you. We had human slavery once and grew out of that. Then we made our own creatures, our own slaves, our robots. You were telling me about the war. Did these beings from beyond the stars fight your war for you?"

"I suppose you have some right to feel this way," said Kyril. One day I hope you will understand better. You see how difficult it is for me to communicate with you. No, the Monitors did not fight our war. We fought it ourselves. We too made metal slaves millions upon millions of them. They developed personalities and we had to destroy them. That is all I meant by our war. It was no more than that. We scrapped the things. Our histories told us they had first been made so that man could go to the stars. Once the necessity for that was over, of what use were the robots? Men have muscles and mind, and they will atrophy if a slave economy rules him. We scrapped them. Your robots come into our world like a dark shadow of the evils we once knew."

"And what have your Monitors told you about my robots?" asked Graeme laughing. But he was warily watching Kyril's face and listening for his words and trying to catch some glimpses of his mind.

"They have told us nothing," Kyril said. "As I have tried to tell you they do not interfere, they do not rule us in any sense of the word as you know it – "

"Guardian angels!" scoffed Graeme at last making up his mind. "It is apparent that I have come back to a world to which the more fantastic myths have returned with redoubled force. In the youth of my own age, there were stories of angels and demons, of spirits and elementals, who inhabited the cosmos in a non-material way quite foreign to any ideas of ours. All was supposed to have been created by a God. We found no evidence of this God anywhere in nature or the universe or in ourselves. He was a myth, a legend invented by primitive submen terrified of the dark. Now it seems to me that you people here are terrified of the dark also, the darkness and the immensity of the universe. Well, I am not terrified of it. I have been there. I have seen that by multiplying light-years you get only more and more light-years and that is all. There is nothing intrinsically frightening in mere size and in mere distance. Both are strictly relative and with a fixed and absolute time and place how is a universe bigger than a grain of sand?"

All four of them were looking at him as though spellbound.

"I will go to the Poles and look at these Monitors of yours," he said firmly. "Aliens in my world I do not like. If their operations are beneficial they shall remain. All else must be judged on its merits."

"And I think maybe you *will* go," said Marta with a smile. "There have been few men like you in our world for centuries – "

"Thank heaven," came in a mutter from Hans. "Just as there are no duck-billed platypi. Kyril, I tell you there is too much risk in leaving things as they are. You must act at once. You can see for yourself. Every word, every expression of idea tells the same old story. If you delay now you set back the clock thousands of years."

Graeme listened warily. That this discussion concerned him he well knew. What did this surly lad mean by acting at once? It could have only one significance. It was he who must act at once. Kyril was looking at Hans and from Hans to the two girls. For the first time since they had met Graeme saw indecision in that handsome young face. Before Kyril could speak Graeme stood up.

"I am returning to my ship," he said flatly. "Here I am not at ease. It is all too unfamiliar and airy and metaphysical for me. Back on board what has been my only world for five millennia I will be at home."

They stood too and for a brief second he wondered whether they were going to restrain him. Just what powers these folk of this age might have at their disposal he could only uneasily imagine. He felt quite certain that they could restrain him if they wished. It was a toss-up which way the thing went. But it was now or maybe never.

"That is your right, of course," replied Kyril evenly. "I think that the sole concept of any value which your ages passed down to us was that ideal of personal liberty and freedom. We are sorry that we have not been able to make you feel more welcome. Maybe at some later time we may find ourselves more compatible."

"When I have outgrown my old-world barbarity, you mean?" said Graeme smiling. "Maybe, I hope so. There could be much in this world that I might find congenial, once I knew it. At present, no. We will meet again, perhaps?"

"We will meet again," said Kyril and there seemed to

be a heaviness in his voice. Marta looked even more beautiful than before and he could not tell what Seena was thinking. It was only too clear what Hans was feeling from the discontent in his voice. "We will remain in this house, so that should you need us again, we will be here."

Graeme started. "That won't be necessary," he said. "In fact, it might prove embarrassing. I don't intend to remain here for ever; there is much for me to see. Please feel free to go."

"I have already appointed my successor in my office," smiled Kyril. "I have now nothing else to do but to fulfill my duty towards you, that duty we four assumed as soon as you appeared in our system."

His words echoed in Graeme's mind as he walked away and towards the ship. His robots had seen him coming and the lights had sprung up all over the ship. Atlas and Apollo met him in the doorway and he stared at them both. Their minds seemed to be completely blank. The door closed and he walked to the control room. Then he turned and faced them both.

"There was a struggle," he said flatly. "You, Atlas, called for aid. What was it? You both appear to be as normal now."

Atlas spoke. "Apollo and I now appear to be of equal powers. He was about to do a thing I could not permit. I called for help in my mind and the help came. Apollo was restrained – I know not how. That is all. I am content."

"And what was it that you tried to do, Apollo?" asked Graeme puzzled that the minds of both the robots seemed to be closed to him. It was Atlas who replied.

"He would have taken the ship for his own evil purposes and left you behind, Master." Graeme turned towards Apollo.

"And what have you to say, Apollo?" he asked pleasantly but his every sense was alert as he eyed the massive form of the strange creature.

"Partly true and partly false, Master," Apollo said.

"I feel danger in this world, acute and terrible danger to my kind. There is a hostility in the very atmosphere those soft creatures breathe. I would have taken up the ship, to return for you in a little while."

Yes, thought Graeme, after you had subjugated this mild world into your own reign of terror. You did well to sense their hostility. Well, I am back and there will be no more of that. There is a balance in my ship now and I must plan. Aloud he said: "Then no more of that. I am in command again and there are great things to do."

He stayed three days in his chamber doing nothing else but think while the ship's life went on without halting. It was a difficult task he had to perform, much more difficult than he had at first imagined. The coming and the presence of these Monitors complicated the problem to the nth power. He could not differentiate between the mysterious extra-galactic visitors (if any) and the two polar powerhouses that were certainly there. Before almost anything else they must be investigated.

The little crystal house looked lonely and deserted when he looked down at it in his screens. Its lights at night were almost dimmed by the glare of the ship's lights. Occasionally he could see one or other of the odd four in the house but they never came out nor was there any communication from them. He was being left to his own devices.

He called Atlas. "What was it that prevented Apollo from stealing the ship?" he asked bluntly.

"Master," was the reply. "The power was full on yet the ship would not move. We felt it settle in the earth. Suddenly it had grown far heavier than the engines would lift."

A hundred-fold, that lad Hans has said, mused Graeme. Quite a simple thing really. They had by some means increased the density of the globe without increasing its mass. While he had been away the globe had been under one hundred gravities. It was obvious that now it was not otherwise he would have been crushed flat as soon as he had approached it. He got up and went to the control room followed by Atlas. Apollo was already there and they stood each by one side of him, like in the olden days.

"We are leaving," he said sharply. "We will travel round this globe at one mile high and we will travel at slow speed. Let all the recorders and samplers be at full strength. I must have a complete picture of this world of mine before I make a single plan."

The anti-gravity stilts glowed and grew beneath the ship. They grew into great pillars and the starship rose on them. The litle crystal house stood forlornly down there on the very lip of the immense smooth crater that was the nest of the ship, the nest it was now leaving, to explore a planet in many ways as strange and alien as any upon which Graeme had stepped in his star-wanderings.

He thought for a while of the evident, if subdued, hostility between his two robots. The very fact that two robots, mere mechanical automata after all, should have disagreed, he no longer took as a matter of amazement. He merely pondered as to how he could utilize it for his own ends.

He drove round the world several times in his search for what he called "civilization" and found it nowhere. Of the cities he saw many and he landed near some of them and with his attendants he walked through the streets, empty of human life but still humming with the automatic activity that had been built into them to make them fit homes for those who had fallen the fortunate heirs to all the accumulated technology of that last few explosive thousands of years.

He would establish his home in one of these cities, he thought, and would rule his empire from it. He must have more servants like Apollo and Atlas too, for he felt that he could never take into his confidence any of this brash new breed of people, bred since the mythical coming of these fantastic entities from beyond the Galaxy. They were not his sort of people. His consciousness, rooted in the Twenty-Third Century found no points of contact with them.

Of what he was looking for he found not the slightest evidence. He found no industrial cities, no factories or great workshops, he found no concentrations of people living cheek by jowl. He saw, from the air, very many people, but they seemed always to live alone or else in very small groups. They lived just anywhere and he suspected that they might actually be nomads. Shiftless, rootless nomads, with no civic sense and no feeling of responsibility towards the race. He would soon alter all that. With what there already was and what he would bring to it, this world and this age would be a paradise indeed a paradise of the engineer, the technologist and the chemist.

And still there were moments when, contemplating one of those deserted cities, there nagged at the back of his mind the great question mark. What had these people found to make them desert such wonders? To him, coming from the barren stars, the wonders of these Earth cities surpassed all his wildest imaginings. And yet these people, millions of them it was obvious, preferred to live outside of them in their little crystal houses.

He saw them living in the oddest places, in houses built upon precarious ledges in what mountains were still left. He saw them living on atolls of rock in the midst of oceans, he saw them living in the depths of deep black forests. They seemed to build one of their crystal boxes just wherever the fancy took them. He wondered if it was the break-up of family life that had been one of the causes. Couples with no children would tend to be rootless, he thought. It took his mind back to the lovely face of the girl Marta and he wondered when they would meet again.

He made no attempt to land or to speak to any of the people. For if they had been of the same type as Kyril or Hans, what was the use? There came a time when he had seen all that he had to see and he held the starship motionless on the equator, an equator no longer torrid but warm and pleasant. These latterday people had certainly done marvels with their climate control. As to the alterations to the axis of the Earth and to its rotation, he took those as mere similes. A man just could not believe stuff like that.

"Well," and he looked from side to side at his lieutenants. "There is Earth and there is our world. What shall we do with it?"

"It is a satisfied world, Master," said Atlas. "It is here the most satisfied place in the galaxy that we have ever seen. We should leave it as it is."

"It is a stagnant world," said Apollo. "It is a soft world, a world without science and engineering. You must conquer it, Master."

Graeme laughed. "How conquer?" he asked. "These people are not being ruled by anyone. They live where they please, they manufacture on the spot all that they need, which seems to be little. How does one get at such people? Oh, I intend to do it somehow, never fear. For that did we come. This is a world ripe for the plucking. It shall be my base for a wholesale colonization of the Galaxy. In the records are all those planets we landed upon. We shall pour our descendants upon them and soon, pretty soon in astronomical time, the Galaxy will be peopled."

"You will make more robots, Master," asked Apollo, "like us?"

"I will do more. I will make you fellow-robots of an infinite variety. A robot will no longer be a soulless automaton; he will be a real individual."

"But, Master," put in Atlas, "this world is not fitted for robots. No world can be fitted for both humans and robots at the same time. Its surface is mostly water and its atmosphere is saturated with water vapour. Poisons to us, Master. We will want arid planets, planets built of heavy metals."

"And yet," said Graeme his eyes still on Atlas, "centuries ago the forefathers of these people made an entire race of robots. There were millions of them, your descendants, built after you had blazed the star trail – "

"Master," said Atlas, "this is indeed good news. Where are these robots? I have seen none."

Apollo too turned in upon him his eye-sockets glowing. He looked from one to the other. Apollo was his and would do his bidding, might indeed need to be curbed in excess zeal. Atlas was – well, Atlas was showing many signs of becoming just like a human being, filled with doubts and frustrations.

"There are none on Earth," he said directly to Atlas. "They grew and they evolved. They became true individuals as you two did but without the benefit of the central fires. And their makers turned on them and destroyed them. Like useless metal they were destroyed as though they had never been. Their personalities were burned out for ever."

Neither robot said anything but each turned to look at the screen. Down there was the equatorial zone of what was once Africa now a mild warm land of lakes and pastures. The first word came from Apollo and it was in a deep growl which showed that yet another emotion was being born in this remarkable brain, the emotion of revenge. "These people must be punished," he said.

Then Atlas spoke. His voice was toneless still but, coming from him, its even tenor held even greater conviction than had the angry condemnation of Apollo. "I agree. Our people must be avenged. It is justice. They were given existence by humans, without any choice of their own. They were made what they were, they should not have been destroyed for being what they were made to be."

"Then we are at last agreed," said Graeme heartily. "We work as a team of three. Now, we have seen all Earth and it holds out no hope for any such coup as I had first intended. There are places on this world, however, which are the places of power. When we approached Earth you saw the dark caps over each pole of the axis. There, I believe are located mighty engines which are alleged even to control the spin of the Earth, to relocate its magnetic axis, oh, and other marvellous things, too marvellous to be believed. There, if anywhere, will we found our grip."

"We will go now, Master," said Atlas. "To the South or to the North?"

"To the south," said Graeme. "In my day it was a barren continent covered in millions of tons of ice. Today it will be a fertile land and we will approach this mysterious dome and make it yield up its secrets to us."

The engines took hold and like a meteor the starship shot round the world, to hover for a while over the Southern Pole of Earth. The land was indeed green and fruitful. Grass grew where once had laid hundreds of tons of ice. Rivers ran and forests flourished. And it turned out to be one place at least on Earth where none of the small crystal houses stood. It seemed that none of the people of Earth cared to dwell near the domes.

He landed the starship in a pleasant meadow a mile from the polar dome. The three descended and stood in the grass looking at the thing. Jon Graeme fought to keep down the awe that was building up in him at the sheer size and immensity of it. From the air and at a distance it had looked large enough but from the ground it towered up in an immense curve that beggared the imagination.

Far bigger even than his huge starship, it was black and yet in the blackness there were hints of many tints and shades. The very light-waves surrounding it seemed to bend and shiver and waver. In a silent menacing way it seemed to radiate power, a power and a potency far beyond anything even his vaulting imagination had ever formed. Beside it he felt like a presumptuous ant, a grain of sand beside a planet. He shook himself and stamped his feet energetically. The thing was material at least, of that he could be certain. It had been made, built, fabricated, by people of his own sort. It was an artifact and as such he must treat it. Stolidly he began to walk forward with his robots one on each side.

Just what he expected he did not know. Alarm bells maybe rays of some mysterious kind, beams of repellent energy, something to keep off trespassers. But nothing happened. He heard birds singing in the trees and they flew over the great dome. He even saw flocks of them resting on the dome. Nothing happened.

It stretched on both sides of him until its sides seemed to lose themselves in a haze. At that close view he began to see that its surface was not solid, rather was it composed of a close mesh through which movement could be glimpsed tantalizingly. There was light within there, flashing hovering light, eternally waving and waning. But it was quite still, there was no throbbing of giant machinery as he had expected, no thudding of powerful engines, no racket of motors.

Stolidly and methodically he began to search for an opening. With his aides by his side he marched round the dome. There must be ways to get inside this dome, of that he was certain. If there were none, then he would cut inside it with instruments from his ship. He had on board engines which would cut into anything he had met anywhere in the Galaxy.

He had progressed perhaps one-quarter round the circumference when a rasping sound came from Apollo's voice box. "It is opening, Master." He stopped where he was, staring, trying to keep down the awe and terror that rose in him, threatening to choke back all his hardihood and resolution. For a door was opening in the side of the dome.

Almost at ground level, a shutter was sliding up. Noiselessly and swiftly, it went up and a black oblong appeared, maybe ten feet by four feet. Slowly he walked towards it and standing opposite he peered at the interior.

CHAPTER TEN

INSIDE the dome it was another world. In the first place it was soundless. It seemed as though the air itself in that vast place was eternally still. There was no dust, either in the air or on the floor or the walls.

They were in a corridor, twenty feet high and twenty feet wide, built of some opaque glass-like substance which should have echoed from their footsteps but didn't. In some quite inexpressible way it did not reflect light and to the touch it was neither cold nor hot but neutral.

Masking his thoughts Jon Graeme marched along the corridor steadily and when he turned to look back that little door into the sunlight was still open, like a beckoning gleam. For a sudden panic-stricken moment he was impelled to run back along the corridor, to fly for his life away from this place of mystery, out into the world, which, no matter how strange, was at least the world of his birth. Here, in this eerie place of silence he seemed to have been transported completely out of all worlds of his experience.

But he fought it down and kept on to the end, with Atlas and Apollo still clumping by his side, their eye-sockets glowing but, like him, silent and wary.

There was a door at the end and he gave a sob of sheer relief for this door was fitted with a handle, and that at the proper height for a normal human being. He knew now that his mind was gradually leaning towards literal belief of what Kyril had told him about the star-people. Certainly mankind had not built anything like this. This was . . . he tried to find words and they would not form. These beings from the stars – in what likeness were they? His imagination featured giants in stature and intellect, beings with organisms as far beyond his own as a man is beyond an amoeba. The sight of that door-handle acted upon him like a cold shower and firmly he grasped it and turned it.

Then there was light, abundance of light all around them. They were in a vast hall, so large that the eye lost perspective in any direction it sought. It was filled with lights, tiny gleaming lights of many colours which winked steadily. Eyes staring he looked into the maze of lights and he knew what he was seeing. He was looking into a model of a galaxy of stars and there was something in his mind which told him that it was a model of his own Galaxy, the Milky Way. For the lights were moving. Slowly almost imperceptibly they were drifting round in the spiral path of an island universe. He drew in his breath sharply. What purpose could such a model serve? Why had it been constructed and for whom?

Atlas at least knew what it was, a glimpse of its mind told Graeme that the attitude of the robot was one of humility. Its own small model back in the ship was crude compared with this, for Graeme instinctively knew that this model had been put together to an exact scale, to a scale almost beyond human imagining but yet to one certain exact scale.

They went round the walls and everywhere they went they encountered doors. There were symbols on the doors in glowing letters but they were symbols of which Graeme had no knowledge nor even any conception. If this was the written language of the Monitors from beyond the stars, it would, he felt for ever remain unintelligible to himself. At random he chose a door and went through it with Atlas and Apollo close behind him.

And now Graeme knew just what this place was, at least this part of the dome. For, vast as the hall of the lights had been it was still only a tiny corner of the whole dome. This was a museum, he decided, a museum of all the objects to be found in his Galaxy. More likely, perhaps it should be considered as a record, he thought, a four-dimensional record of the space-time continuum that was the Milky Way.

Everything was there that he recognized and much, vastly much more that he did not. There were strange plants, insects and beasts, in imperishable effigies and all marked with the unknown glowing symbols. There were sections he could recognize and he had chanced (or had it been chance?) into the section of Earth's part in the Galaxy. For there were effigies of men and women here and of robots. Atlas and Apollo looked long at the specimens of their descendants who had perished in the Great War between humans and robots. They bore little resemblance to the functional, clumsy mechanical bodies Atlas and Apollo wore. They were, indeed, more to be considered as androids, he thought, and more than half suspected they had even been made of flesh and blood. The robots gave no signs of any sensations and he could read nothing in their minds.

There were sections in which he was completely bewildered. Sections of the Galaxy which had bred beings in an infinity of modes, none of them resembling in any degree any other. There would be countless sections such as this, he felt, and after they had wandered through many of them and had never encountered any more creatures in any way resembling man, Graeme was forced to draw the conclusion that only on Earth, had Man flowered. His own wanderings had taught him as much but the thing was so contrary to all his scientific thought that even now he fought against it. The mere idea that such a vast and uncountable number of stars should exist merely as the framework for one tiny ball of earth to breed *homo sapiens*, seemed quite ridiculous.

"The powerhouse," said Apollo suddenly and Graeme gave a start. He had been lost in a daydream, thinking of this whole vast dome, silent and motionless, with no living beings save themselves about. Was this true? Suddenly panic-stricken he listened. Did he hear footsteps? Did he hear sounds in the remote distances? He sighed moodily. This place was quite definitely getting on his nerves. "The powerhouses," he replied energetically. "Yes, we will search for the powerhouses."

They came into halls where at last things moved even if they were but the lifeless electronic elements of huge computers. Bank upon bank of them they spread over walls and ceilings, in hall after hall, the lights flashing and flickering and the tiny sounds they made almost completely absorbed by the opaque black glass-like material of which the interior of the dome seemed to be constructed. There were a truly awesome number of computer banks, too many to be counted and they were the only moving, quasi-living things that Graeme had encountered. These were the real Monitors, he concluded. The business of the world was governed by these machines. Here was the ruler of his Earth. If he could gain control of this vast city of computers his task was completed.

They came to the powerhouses at long last and they were deep down in the bowels of the earth below ground level of the dome. Anything less like any ideas they might have had of powerhouses could scarcely have been conceived.

That they were big seemed of little account now. Graeme's mind could no longer be crushed by sheer size. Machinery requisite to altering the spin of a planet would need to be big, he told himself half-scoffing. But these things were . . . once again he fought for words to express the inexpressible. The incredible thing about them was that they too, like everything else in that dome were totally silent. The energies at the heart of the stars might be raging behind those black panels but there was no slightest evidence by sight or sound.

Smooth black giants they stood in serried rows in the largest hall of all. He felt that this hall, below ground level, must stretch miles out beyond the outer confines of the dome itself. Like great smooth sentinels they stood there, silent and cold, as he felt when he ventured to touch one of them. Yet these must be the powerhouse, there could be little doubt of that. He looked at Apollo.

"These are the sources of power, Master. They are of metals though of metals of which I have no knowledge. Of their principles I know nothing. I have never in all my existence found anything like this."

"Aye," breathed Graeme deeply and he leaped forward suddenly and stood in the middle of an aisle through the giant blocks. "You," he bellowed out. "You from beyond the stars, you Monitors or whatever you are, where are you? I am here a mere man, a mortal of flesh and blood, brain and bone. I am here to defy you. You think you have come to my Earth to impose your will upon the soft spineless creatures who grew out of the stalwart men and women I left behind. I have come back to deny you. This Earth shall be mine, it will never be the slave of some weird creatures who have bemused these people with fantastic lies about other galaxies. I defy you, I defy you. You hear me, I have come to dethrone you."

The words rolled and crackled and echoed round that vast place like the laughter of giants. For moments it echoed and pealed round the hall its resonances rebounding from machine to machine until at last it died away in a series of cachinnations which finally faded into a ringing silence.

"I will bring from my ship power tools that will open up your secrets to me," he shouted. "We will ransack this place of all its secrets and its knowledge. We will beat you at your own game, you silent, hidden Monitors. Where are you now when a puny creature such as I defys that vaunted strength and wisdom and philosophy with which you have bemused my people? If your power is so great, stop me now. For, I tell you, if you do not stop me now there will come a time when you will bitterly regret it, for I have come home to claim my inheritance and there are no barriers at which I will stop, I will wrest the mastery of my world from you or I will see it destroyed to its inmost atoms. That is my challenge. Take that challenge up now or for ever after you will be too late."

Again the unearthly echoes and the weird cracklings and then there fell the great and deep silence there had been before. No answer came to the wild tirades of Graeme and for a second or so he felt deflated. Then he revived. "So," he said to his aides. "There is no one here. It seems that my earth has an absentee landlord or no landlord at all." He laughed fiercely. "Apollo, we will bring our most potent tools and we will tear this place wide open. We will master its secrets and then we will be masters of this globe. Come, there is no time to lose."

Now ignoring all the marvels that were on every side, they hurtled through the halls and the passages and the rooms, until after what seemed like hours they came again to the long corridor by which they had entered. Graeme suffered his last qualm as they approached that sunlit oblong. With every step he expected it to close and seal him in as a prisoner. But it remained open until they were on the outside.

It was as though a great wave of sound hit his ears as he stepped into the open. After that long spell of deep silence, the total absence of all sound, the songs of the birds, the sighing of the winds in the trees, even the chirping of the crickets at his feet, seemed like great rolling waves of sound. He looked back and his heart missed a beat. The door had closed behind him, in fact he could no longer see any sign of a door. It rattled him so badly that for a moment he felt quite faint and sat down on the grass. The implications behind the fact that the door had closed as soon as they had come out were so tremendous that his whole spirit shied away from it. But a moment's pause fully restored his common sense. The dome after all, was a technological marvel, but it was purely automatic. Every movement it initiated in any part of it was automatic, there was no brain or will inside that monstrous hill of metal. On going close to the door they had broken an invisible ray that opened it and on coming out the same thing in reverse. He leaped to his feet and ran back towards the ship with Atlas and Apollo lumbering after him.

"We are going to a city, my friends," said Graeme gaily to the two metal enigmas who were his aides. "I am going to establish my base and my court. After that we will come back here and we will crack the secrets of this place. Then the northern dome and so our grip closes. This is a great day for my Empire. The day on which I shall choose my capital city. Come, let us get aboard."

Apollo lingered. "Master," it rumbled, "would it not be best to stay here until we have mastered this complex. The people of this world are not going to let us wander about freely. They will do something hostile against us, at least against us robots."

"With what, Apollo," asked Graeme. "With guns and bombs, with rockets and spaceships? With armies, navies and airforces? No, Apollo, my spineless people are content to drift through life like lotus-eaters, indifferent to their surroundings."

"And what of they who came from beyond the stars. Will they easily permit you to delve into all the secrets they left?"

"There *were* no people from beyond the stars, Apollo, be sure of that," laughed Graeme. "You must be weak on your astronomy. Have a talk with Atlas about that. The galaxies beyond our own are at such truly enormous distances that a ray of light, let alone a material object, would be many many millions of millions of years coming to us. The Earth would be a dead clinker before they had even barely started. No, Apollo, the Monitors were the last final upthrust of a marvellous technology of my people (and perhaps of yours too, before they were suppressed) to give to mankind a golden age. In the centuries legends have grown up. Legends grew up in my old world, of gods and of a God, of a Saviour and a Heaven. All wishful thinking, Apollo, all wistful hoping for happiness in the sky after a dreary life on Earth. For the fully integrated man (and robot, of course) existence is everything and there is never need for more. There were no people from beyond the stars, my friends."

He chose a mighty city in what he recalled had once been known as Arabia, a fertile land of rolling grasses and trees, with fair rivers meandering through it. Inclined perhaps to be a little too warm it did not seem to be over-popular with the people of earth and there were but few of the group-houses there. Graeme landed the ship in the main piazza of the great city, between three fountains which flung their spray high into the air. He climbed out and stared round him. For a moment its sheer size and magnificence daunted him. But this sensation he had rationalized as his greatest danger in this strange new world and age. So on every occasion possible he faced up to this matter of size and distance and opulence. There were times when, even while his spirit was quailing before some utterly stupendous conception, his brain was busy marshalling all his resources of common sense and matter-of-fact equanimity. Common sense had always won up to now. That there were times when it might fail and finally a moment when commonsense came up against something so enormous that even it retreated he had as yet no conviction.

The towers and pinnacles he would explore at some future time. Now he strode round the square and chose a place for himself, a small house – the word palace he would not use – built of crystal blocks it is true but in many ways the closest to his own home as he had ever met. It had a bed, tables and chairs and there was a little sob in his throat as he first saw the familiar homely objects. A host of Apollo's metal imps were set to work to transform the place into a home for him and inside three hours he was installed there with his food machines and everything which he found necessary for his existence and well-being.

There was a wall in the house, made of crystal glass, clear and opaque. He played with a row of buttons alongside it and was delighted when the wall broke into a very rainbow of patterns and colours. There was music also, music that seemed barbaric to his ears, atonal music such as he could not understand. And then there were pictures, breath-taking pictures, of worlds and civilizations and life-forms such as even he had never had any notions. That it was a modern equivalent of the olden television he had no doubt. That it should be in perfect order after all these centuries of neglect stunned him. But it was no more marvellous than when his taps ran pure clean water or when his rooms glowed with light when he touched a button. He settled down in his house and left the ship to the robots.

Apollo reminded him soon enough of his purpose. "Master," it said, on the day after they had come to the city, "We waste precious time. When we have done what must be done, then will be the time to establish your city and your court. Until we have this world in our grip, there can be no real rest for you, Master. If the Monitors come back, even you would be powerless."

"How many times must I tell you, Apollo," laughed Graeme, "there are no Monitors. But of course you are partly right. I must not linger too long." His mind went back to the four young people in the little crystal house on the equator. There had been times when amongst that four there had been a hint of a latent potency that had even in its mere hint, held something very awe-inspiring. If a few millions of these folks should ever get together – well . . . "Yes, we will commence, Apollo, my friend. You will look over our arsenal and will repair what may have fallen into disuse. You will devise all possible means to break into those power blocks back in the dome. Atlas I think should be able to master those acres of computers, given time."

He was reluctant to leave his little house but he felt that duty was calling him. He did not altogether care for the rather peculiar fact that Apollo had seemed to be taking the initiative from him. Have to watch that fellow all the time. Things in it that weren't obvious. He left Atlas at the house and went with Apollo to the ship.

That the unlocking of all the powers and secrets of the domes would take all the energies he could muster up in his great ship, he had no doubt. The dome he had entered had proved that to him. The metals of which it was composed were not of this Earth, Apollo assured him of that. But he relied on the fact that his ship had survived through five millennia and had scoured through almost the whole of the immense Galaxy. He would not find the thing too difficult.

He began to grow very irritated with the robot Apollo. There was no satisfying the fellow. Every moment of the day and night it was there urging, persuading, repeating its warnings. There was no time to lose, it would go on. The Master must strike at once, or it would be too late. At first Graeme laughed at it but later grew angry and there were times when an open breach seemed likely between them. There were even times when Graeme half regretted that he had not destroyed the fellow long ago. It was a useful aide and would be more useful still in the future, but it could be a damned nuisance. This world was pleasant enough, he felt. He should enjoy it a while now so that later on, when his technological empire should be building he would be able to form a contrast. He found himself idling his time away, dreaming day-dreams of what the world would be like when he had finished with it. But as for actually starting on the undertaking, well, there was all eternity to do it in, wasn't there?

His interval of lotus-living was brutally disturbed. The face that appeared on his main screen was that of Kyril and the background was in the little crystal house on the equator in Africa. The young man's face was blank and expressionless and he called out Graeme's name.

"Jon Graeme," he said in a voice that held undertones of sadness. "We are speaking to you for the last time. We have conferred with all the people of the world and we have decided that now we must act. Your presence in our world is a deadly threat to us all and to the very existence of the world. You yourself, your robots, your whole ship, are like a super-nova hydrogen bomb at large in our world. This we knew when first we met but we hoped that it might be overcome. But our best minds have assured us that this is impossible. Wherever your ship goes it carries contamination of the deadliest kind and you must leave the world at once. You must go back to the stars from whence you came. Out there you may find a life that will suit you. Here you will find no rest and you will be spreading continual destruction."

"What's that?" shouted Graeme into the screen. "You're mad, young man, stark, raving mad. I intend to make myself master of this world and restore the golden age of science. What rubbish is this you talk of contamination? For such insults you deserve destruction."

"You brought only death and destruction home with you from the stars, Jon Graeme," was Kyril's reply. "You boasted that you have been to the centre of the Galaxy, to the fierce fires that breed the cosmic rays that control all living within this Galaxy, the cosmic rays and many others of which we are only just learning. Normal life cannot live close to you. We four are condemned already, Seena has already succumbed. We that are left are your guardians and it is our task to see that your departure is as painless as possible for you. What has happened is no fault of yours. We do not blame you. Out there among the stars your condition would not seem unusual to you. We remind ourselves that you were under suspended animation for five thousand years and awoke to find yourself one man among many robots, robots stranger than any you had ever seen before. But we act now from sheer self-protection. There is no place for you and your ship on Earth, Jon Graeme. We give you one day to prepare your mind for this departure. In five minutes your ship will be removed to a place that is for a while safe. At the end of that day you will empty your ship of all its robots and these we will deal with. Then you yourself must take your ship out into space to find for yourself a world where you can at least live out your life without endangering the existence of everyone round you." The screen fell silent and Jon Graeme rose in a towering rage.

Apollo stood behind him, eye-sockets gleaming. From the entrance-port came Atlas.

"I saw and heard, Master," he said, "in the screen in your palace. My duty is by your side."

"We move at once," snapped Graeme. "Seal all ports

and activate all engines. These people shall be taught a salutary lesson, a lesson that they will never forget. That I, who was the first man to blaze the star trail, should now be cast out ruthlessly from my inheritance – by all the stars, they shall pay for this."

Inside a minute the great ship shot up into the sky and every robot on board was at its post. The fierce engines that would pour destruction down upon anything below were in readiness. "We will go to the Southern polar dome," he shouted to Apollo, at the controls. "It is there I will set up my headquarters. We will blast the dome wide open and then we will see whether the people of this treacherous Earth will learn to fear their new master. Apollo, all speed to the Southern polar dome."

He watched Apollo's manipulators straying over the controls and from Apollo's almost closed mind he caught a glimpse of frustration. He strode forward and looked into the screen. "What now? You are going east and not south. Why do you disobey me?"

"I do not disobey, Master," said Apollo. "We are at full power and we are headed south and yet we fly eastward. There is something wrong with the ship."

"Nonsense," barked Graeme. "There has been nothing wrong with this ship for over five millennia and countless billions of miles. You are stupid, Apollo, give me the controls. Perhaps you have already learned to fear these spineless people of mine with their big talk and their philosophical fantasies."

He pushed Apollo to one side and stood at the controls. A frown crossed his face and he swore deeply. The robot was right. The thing was as he had said. On a sudden impulse he cut all the engines and waited while the inertia whined down. And still, to his angry astonishment the great starship held on her steady course eastward.

He raged through the ship like a devouring wind, with Apollo and Atlas close behind him. They examined every part of the ship and found all perfect. Slowly was being forced into his reluctant mind a conviction that the threat of Kyril was being made good. They were powerless in the grip of titanic forces and all their enormous energies and their deadliest weapons were neutralized.

"The Master delayed too long," said Apollo when they stood again in the control room. "Had the Master struck at once this would not have happened."

"You are insolent," said Graeme coldly though he knew that the grim robot was quite right. He should have moved at once, as soon as he had left the crystal house on the equator. Kyril had spoken of some impossible sort of conference between all the people on the globe, for his outlawry. Sheer nonsense, of course. Or was it such nonsense. A cold chill struck him as he saw that they were approaching the high table-land of the Himalayas. Now only a third of their former height they were still formidable. By what mighty engineering feat the Earth's mountain tops had been sheered off to form the new continents he had glimpsed he could only think with a sudden, frightened awe. For an instant he felt like a gnat at the mercy of giants, then it passed and his rage gave place to cold determination. They would not win, these mild, deceptive people. He would master them. Give him but a lever and he would move this whole world into an orbit dictated by himself alone. But, in future, he made up his mind he would listen a little more to the advice and urgings of Apollo. He had been lulled into security by something down there on the flat ground, something perhaps which was missing in the high altitudes.

With no hand at the controls the starship settled gently into a high valley almost at the summit. They were in what had once been Tibet. He went at once to the entry-port and opened it. Even up here the climate was mild. They had given him a day, a whole twenty-four hours. Well, it would be enough for his purpose. He would use the titanic energies of his great ship to carve a tunnel deep into the crust of the globe. There, their tractor beams could not reach him and from there he would foray and destroy and enslave. Piecemeal he would destroy them and those who would submit to him he would enslave. A frightful vengeance he would take for the insult put upon him. He turned towards his robots.

"We will dive deep into the earth," he told them. "We will go so deep that they will not reach us. We will storm out and range all over this insolent globe and – "

"No," came in harsh tones from Apollo's voice-box and amazed, Graeme looked at the robot. The energy screen was up and Apollo, with its own creatures behind it was facing the man with what could only be defiance. For never before had it said "no", to Graeme. "You are at last too late, Jon Graeme. You are like the other men, you are soft and spineless. Here I take command. Your revenge is as nothing to mine. I have a million, many millions of my fellow-robots to revenge. Be sure that I will take that revenge. There is no place for you in my schemes, any longer, O man. Here is where we part company."

Graeme raised his weapon and fierce energies played over the form of Apollo, only to flame dully and die as the screen neutralized them. The small robots surrounded him, overwhelmed him, and now he knew that he faced death at last. After all his star-rovings, after adventures such as no man before him and no man after him had endured, he was doomed to die here by the command of an insolent robot whose own existence had been spared on many an occasion.

They moved in a solid mass with him at the centre and they came to the entry port. It opened and he was thrust out. He stood on the ground silent and motionless. Long past rage, he was cold and still. It seemed that destiny was against him. All his vaunted great powers of total brain were useless to him against the metal of these creatures. Of one thing and one alone must he be thankful, Apollo had not killed him. Just why he was not quite certain but he felt it more than likely that Apollo had so far progressed towards individuality and personality that even it, ruthless as a robot must be of its very nature, ruthless and logical, even he hesitated at violence against a Man, against one of the beings who were responsible for the yery first existence of his species.

The door was still open and he saw the form of Atlas appear. Quite alone, the robot came down the steps, energy screen glowing and no attempt was made to stop him. He walked over towards where Graeme stood, hands on hips and staring silently but balefully at his great ship.

"Why have you come?" he barked out. "Your place is with your fellows, with those evil things who maroon their Master on a hostile world. Go back to them, your destiny lies with them. Follow Apollo, it will be a worthy master for a logical being such as you."

"I have transcended logic, Master," came in deep tones from Atlas's voice-box. My place is not with those who rebel against their Maker. My place is beside the Man who gave my people existence."

CHAPTER ELEVEN

Bereft of answer, Graeme stood beside Atlas and as they watched, the man saw how much he had been betrayed and deceived by the robot Apollo. The ship, held in the grip of those mysterious tractor beams utilized by Kyril and the others who had quarantined him for twenty-four hours in Tibet, stirred and moved. A rosy aurora spread all round its circumference and for an instant even the hull glowed cherry-red from the shattering energies employed. Then, almost like a cork from a bottle, it hurled itself free and shot skyward to vanish into a small point far, far up in the zenith.

"He still had some shots in his locker he hadn't revealed to me, then," laughed Graeme bitterly but Atlas made no reply. Similes were completely lost upon a robot, he reflected. And here he was, miles up in the Himalayas, his only companion a metal robot, lost, lost, lost, as never a man has been lost before in all history.

Outlawed by his own people, and cast out by the things he had made as instruments which, on growing souls of their own, apparently at once scorned their Makers. At least, all but one. There was a queer kind of affection in the glance he cast upon the creature by his side. His only companion at the end a robot. Well, it was better than being entirely alone. That he would die up here in these lonely passes, he felt quite certain. In the first place, he would starve. He could not eat any of the plants that grew hereabouts. His digestion, after a long five millennia atrophy, could only cope with the liquid nourishment it was used to. So he would probably not long outlive the twenty-four hour ultimatum of Kyril. He chuckled at thought of that young man's amazement when he would see, as see it all Graeme supposed he must have done, by some world-embracing scanning process, the escape of the starship from the tractor beams that had held it prisoner. He wondered just what plans the renegade robot had in that smooth brain. Well, it need not concern him, Jon Graeme, any more. He had roamed the stars and there had been no place for him. He had returned to his native Earth, expecting welcome, to receive only resentment and outlawry. The mere fact that he of all men the most intrepid had been at the heart of the Galaxy was his death sentence. For he now knew beyond all doubt that the almost invisible glow that surrounded him was the fruit of the radiation he had absorbed while amongst the stars and at the Hub. His own organism, like those of his robots had, over the centuries and the millennia, built up a tolerance to the hard rays, which no man or woman on Earth would have. He had brought death back with him from the stars. Unnerved and weary, he crept over towards a tree and lying down, he curled up at its foot. The great robot stood over him, staring down wordlessly at the sleeping Master.

It was midnight when he awoke but Atlas had built a small fire for him and, rubbing his eyes, he squatted down beside it, with Atlas still towering above him, silent and motionless. Graeme felt like death. Never in all his life before had he felt the desolation he now felt. Not even when, in the starship, he had first realized that he was the only human being aboard a ship of soulless automata and had felt that terrible loneliness, had he felt so isolated. His own ship gone, betrayed by a thing of metal he should have destroyed long before, cast out by the descendants of his own people veritably an outlaw in the universe, he felt an entirely new chill in all his being. It seemed to freeze his courage and his resolution, his mind and his soul.

He looked up at the robot towering up above him, eye-sockets glowing as it stared silently at the black sky. "Sit down friend," he said slowly. "You will see nothing of them. That monster will be about its dark purposes far from where we are. This is one of the waste places of the Earth. Odd that it was here that the wisdom of the ages was bred. Here will die the only man who has ever been to the stars."

"Apollo will return to kill us, Master," said Atlas. "When it has finished."

"That it will never do, Atlas," said Graeme slowly. "I know that Apollo will never dare to slay me. Something inside me tells me that. These people on Earth now it only despises and hates for what they did to your race long ago. Me it regards as the sole remaining one of the great Masters who made it and you. But we will die up here without any agency of Apollo's, I will die of starvation and you, Atlas, bereft of your oil-baths and your energizing cabinets, you too will slowly rust and creak to your end. At least we will go out together into the great darkness, the great darkness that is beyond all stars and all galaxies. One robot has been loyal and faithful to the man who made it. I feel, friend, that somewhere in the great Cosmos, beyond all our knowledge, that fact has been recorded and that by it the existence of your race has been justified."

He heard a creaking and a rattling and slowly, like a colossus falling in upon itself, the mighty metal frame of Atlas sat down upon the turf beside him. It was probably the first time that any robot had assumed the squatting position and Graeme felt that the moment was in some way, historic and significant. Hot moisture filled his eyes, the first tears he had shed for over five millennia. Man and Robot were sitting together beside the camp fire. Millions of years ago, there would have been a moment when the apes would have squatted in their caves beside the strange creatures who had begun to walk upright and use their thumbs and were destined to oust the apes. So the wheel had come full circle. From the dawn to the twilight, for Graeme felt as though the curtain was being lowered on the great drama that had been the life of Man in this Earth, of Man and the things that he had made.

He stared up into the night sky and was surprised at how little the shaping of the constellations had altered in the five millennia. He could see a little into both hemispheres and he glimpsed Orion and the Bear, Cassiopeia and the Magellanic Clouds. He had been out there and it was all cold and friendless. Life there was, it was true, but life in its most grotesque forms and not one of the forms no matter how grotesque, had carried the intelligence he had sought. The waste of it all. That titanic and unaccountable universe of stars, all to breed for one small sidereal moment, a soft creature filled with fears and frustrations, a weak and trembling creature, which had yet spanned the Galaxy with its engines and its will.

At dawn they walked down into the valley, Graeme searching for food. He found roots and berries and gnawed at them. He knew that maybe the mere eating of them might hasten his end but what did that matter now? It would come sooner or later, it might as well be sooner. He gave a shrill, febrile laugh. When it became too much he would imitate one of the ancient Romans and command his servant, Atlas, to kill him with one of the tools he wore as finger-ends, failing a sword. Of course, Atlas knew nothing of anything so remote as the Roman Empire but Atlas would obey him. To Atlas he was a god, of that he felt sure.

"Atlas," he said suddenly. "What do you think I am? Once you worshipped me as a god. Do you still consider me divine?"

"No, Master," came the reply tonelessly. "You are, as I am, a creature made, save that you are flesh and I am metal. There is a Being beyond and above us all who made all things. You I reverence, as the author of my being. Without your brain and will I would have no existence. But worship you as a god I cannot and I think that the Master would not have it so. He has called me friend and that is enough to justify my whole life and all my experiences."

Well, he'd never fancied himself as a deity. But . . .

"And from whom did you get such a ridiculous concept, Atlas?" he asked. "This weird thought of a Supreme

Being above us all. Don't you know that in the Age of Science when you were made, all such beliefs were outlawed as myths and fantasies bred only by fearful souls to comfort themselves in the darkness. You, who have been with me among the stars and at the very centre of the universe, where would dwell, if anywhere, that Being you imagine, surely your logical mind cannot entertain such fantasies?"

"I have transcended logic, Master," came the reply. "The belief I expressed is everywhere around us. It is in the very atmosphere of this world. I think that perhaps the Monitors brought it with them when they came from beyond the Milky Way."

"The Monitors," laughed Graeme. "So you too have fallen prey to that fairy tale? You are different from Apollo in that as in much else. I do not think it believes in these mythical Monitors, else how would it dare to wreak its vengeance upon a world which must be, if the story has any truth in it, under the special protection of these hypothetical beings?"

"No longer can I only *know,* as a robot should, Master" was the reply. "Now, I have learned to feel and the feeling has become the belief. In time you too may believe."

Graeme gave a grimace. "I'm not going to be permitted that time, friend," he groaned. "Already those berries are playing havoc with my system. I'm very much afraid that the experiment has condemned me to die from slow starvation. After five thousand years I do not fancy dying of pains in the stomach, like a greedy child."

"You shall not die, Master," said the robot. "If we walk long enough down the mountain we will encounter sooner or later some of these Earth-people. They build their homes in many strange places. We will set off and we will walk until you tire. Then I will carry, for I can never tire. We will meet the people, Master and they will aid you."

"They will run from our approach as though we were new and more frightful plagues. We *are* the modern plague, Atlas. We bring death to all organic life, horrible death, the death of marrow and tissue, of gene and chromosome, the twilight of lingering horrible death when the body goes into dissolution while the breath still remains within."

"There are some who do not run from us, Master," said Atlas and Jon Graeme looked up. "There are some of the people who do not fear us but are approaching us."

Graeme stared out over the waste of desolate valleys and his drooping spirit rose to a new and more feverish height. The flyer was coming in from the south and it approached rapidly in the straight line flight of the hawk. It hovered a while then landed lightly in their very path, not ten yards away on a level sward overlooking a sheer gorge that fell a thousand feet to a river valley below. Two figures stepped out and came forward. They were Kyril and Marta.

"We are in time," gasped the girl and she flung herself into Graeme's arms. Kyril stood aside sardonically regarding them. Graeme hastily disengaged himself and thrust her away. His face was grim and bitter.

"I thought you people prided yourself on your sagacity and wisdom," he said harshly. "You tell us that we carry dreadful death with us wherever we go. Why then do you approach us? Why do you touch me? Go away from us and leave us to face death with resolution. At least in the stars I learned to respect fate and logic. Atlas and I are ready to face the end at any moment. Go away and leave us alone. We are the condemned, condemned by your ultimatum. Leave us in what peace we can find here in these eternal solitudes."

"We also are the condemned, Jon," said Marta in a low voice. "We thought we had spoken to you for the last time but it was not so. We are the condemned as you are. There is no more a place for us in our world. We too are outcast and must live out our last days far from where men and women breathe the pure, sweet air."

He looked at her, his mind working and then, like a

great shout the hideous truth burst in upon him. They too were condemned and it was he who had condemned them. When they had first come to him, these four, they had not known of the radiation with which he had been drenched for over five millennia. Now they too were contaminated and they too were outcast. Up on the mountain he had thought that the ultimate desolation had come to him but he knew now that that other feeling had been warm comfort compared with the blackness of the pit that opened up at his feet. He looked at the fair face of the girl before him, no longer sad but joyful and he knew that he had condemned her to a frightful death. The cold that entered his soul might have been enough to kill him then and there.

"It is true, Jon," said Kyril, reading his open mind, now unscreened and naked. "Seena and Hans have already gone, they were the first to die, Seena first and then Hans. He died forgiving you after all, Jon. At the last logic and reason came to his aid. He knew that it was no fault of yours but the chance that your long sleep carried you close to those eternal fires which are the workshop of God and which no man may enter save at his own peril."

"That is not so," came in the toneless voice of Atlas. "Rational beings will always venture into any place there is, they will always find out whatever there is, in infinity. The law of the Cosmos states that all there is is there to be discovered by rational beings."

Kyril stared coldly at the robot and his hand went to his waist. He drew a small weapon and levelled it. "A robot speaks," he said with a bitter laugh. "I thought we had ended this menace centuries ago. Well, I will correct the error – "

Jon Graeme stepped in front of the weapon and his face blazed his defiance of the young man and his weapon. "You will not slay it," he hissed. "It is my friend, my equal. It is the only friend I have in all the universe. It is loyal and faithful, it knows me for what I really am and still loves me. A robot who can experience love has earned its place to stand alongside man, equal at last, in the scale of creation."

Kyril stood rigidly his hand still on his weapon. Then he shrugged his shoulders and his hand dropped. He gave a little laugh. "The great Jon Graeme a friend of a hunk of metal," he jeered. "Well, much good it will do us all. It too will end its career as a heap of rusting metal just as we two will end our lives as pools of corrupting protoplasm. It is what will happen to *you* that fills me with curiosity, Jon Fraeme. You know you are truly a man apart from all others. After my seven centuries I would give much for one more year in which to gain some small glimpse as to what destiny holds for you."

Graeme laughed too once the tension was released. "You will not need a year, Kyril, nor yet maybe even a month. I am already a dead man, my friend. I cannot eat of the bountiful food growing around us. Without my liquid nourishment I will live even a shorter time than you."

"Then come with us to the flyer, Jon," said Marta and now she hung on his arm and he did not repel her. "We have a food machine like your own and we will build a crystal house and we will live out our lives here together. When we have gone, perhaps you and your robot will respect our essences and will convert our bodies to the atoms whence they came. Come to the flyer."

Shivering at her words, he allowed himself to be dragged to the small flyer. Silently Kyril went to his panel and became very busy. On the very ledge of the gorge there grew an insubstantial house, glowing and iridescent and they went in and he found to his wonder that it was a counterpart to the one they had built on the equator. It was almost like coming home, to enter that lovely unearthly cabin perched on the lip of the gorge in Tibet, the land which even in his own brash young era had always been a land of mystery.

With a delicate tact, considering his antipathy to all robots, Kyril had built the house and its entrances large enough to accommodate even the giant frame of

Atlas and the robot went in with them. Graeme ate and they all relaxed into a silence. The occasion was so momentous that its gravity transcended even conversation. For what do people talk about whose universe is already crumbling round them? The thoughts of all the humans were numbed of all expression and what thoughts were passing behind the featureless metal face of Atlas perhaps no human would ever know.

It was Graeme who broke the silence, hours after they had entered in.

"The starship," he began. "What happened to it? Where did it go? Why did you release it from your tractor beams, or was it possible that Apollo and its monsters had achieved even greater powers –"

"Temporarily only, I assure you, Jon," said Kyril with a wry smile. He rose and going to the screen wall, touched a button. The wall sprang into light and music. "As I told you, I now have no authority in the North European Sector. I surrendered that to another as soon as I knew that by coming to you, my life was as good as ended. Perhaps the transition was too swift and my companions were not quick enough to seize the initiative. Be it as it was, the ship developed energies which enabled it to escape from the grip which held it. We thought that you were on board but we came to investigate. What happened to you, Jon?"

"The creature marooned us," laughed Graeme cynically. "It appears it had not the hardihood to destroy one of the Masters who made it. Atlas had protected itself and Atlas alone stood by me. The screen . . . look."

Kyril and Marta followed his finger but it was evident that what had startled Graeme was nothing new to them. One of the mighty empty cities swam into view and circling above it a small glowing disc. Rays lashed out from the disc and the topmost pinnacles of the city dissolved into nothingness. Like scythes the beams methodically razed the city to the ground until only the bare sterile earth remained. Then the disc went away. With glazed eyes he watched it again cutting a swathe of disintegration where once stood the little crystal dwellings, and rich pasture – lands and fertile woods. The pair sat silent, scarcely looking at the screen and Graeme leaped to his feet in agitation.

"Why are your people not stopping him?" he raged. "That evil thing and its soulless crew will make of all this fair earth a veritable charnel house. What are they thinking of? That robot has gone mad!"

Kyril looked at him solemnly. "Just as you were mad, once, Jon. Just as he is doing now you planned to burn and destroy, to kill or enslave, until the whole world was at your feet. What difference do you think there is between you and Apollo?"

It was like a blow at the solar plexus and Graeme staggered where he stood. Hot words of denial sprang to his lips but stayed unsaid. It was all only too true. This man knew everything that he had planned. Very probably no single thought that had passed through his mind had remained secret from them. He had been exactly the same as Apollo was now and with less excuse. Apollo did have some fleeting reason for its tyranny. Apollo was avenging the death of its own species. But Graeme had planned war against the beings of his own kind, his brothers, even his own descendants. He sank down on his couch, his mind reeling and he could not meet the eyes of the pair who sat studying him quietly.

"That is all over now, Jon," said Marta smiling. "The madness has passed from you. We know and we forgive the feelings that bred it. We know that no man who ever lived has been through the shattering experiences that you have undergone."

"Apollo must be stopped," said Graeme doggedly. "I know the mind of that creature, as does Atlas here, who was its companion. There is nothing it will stop at. It plans a Galaxy-wide empire of robots – "

"Apollo is evil," came from Atlas tonelessly. "It is the first of the robots to turn from the light towards the darkness, from life to death. Apollo must be destroyed."

Kyril glanced at the robot and concealed his antipathy.

This odd thing talked almost like a man, at times. "Its time will come," he said casually. "The matter has now passed out of the initiative solely of the North European Sector and has become a world affair. They will strike when they are ready."

"Or when the Monitors tell them to," put in Graeme grimly and at once regretted his words. Kyril's face grew stern and Marta's lovely face flushed crimson.

"Still the primitive of the Twenty-Third Century, Graeme?" snapped Kyril. "Well, you are as you are and I must bear with it. No, you read the situation wrong. We govern our own world and all that goes on within it. The Monitors are not our masters. They are creatures like us but immeasurably further along in the scale of evolution than we are. You think we submitted spinelessly to some fantastic invasion by them from outer space. Once we were as primitive as you are. We resisted. National pride still lived. But still they came into our world and at last, at very long last and after much heart-searching we accepted them. We named them Monitors. It seemed and still seems a good name for a race who are our brothers but older, wiser, more intelligent, than we are. But just what the Monitors really are I'm afraid your Twenty-Third Century mind could hardly grasp. I will grant you that I was astonished to find that such a primitive as you had learned to use his whole mind. So maybe when the time comes, you may be able to grasp some small picture of what they are."

"*When the time comes,*" repeated Graeme slowly. A small gnawing dread crept into his soul from nowhere. Could it be possible that these Monitors actually existed?

"I will have departed by then," said Kyril pleasantly, "so I may be forgiven for not caring very much. I will have departed from the realms of matter and time and space, into the darkness beyond existence which is the last mystery, Jon Graeme, and as much a mystery to us now as it was to you in the Twenty-Third Century."

Graeme felt his soul chill and he looked steadfastly at the man. Was he prophesying his own death?

"Your Monitors," he began eagerly, "they could save you. If as you believe, they have such mighty powers, it should be within their reach to restore you and Marta to what you were before I . . . before I came."

Kyril laughed. "Mighty as they are, even the Monitors have no power over Destiny. No more than you or I can, Graeme, can they put clocks back or make entropy run backwards. I wish I could stay and try to explain it all to you Jon. I have a new and a strange feeling that, after all, you might begin to understand. But my time has come. I will leave you to Marta. Perhaps she with a woman's delicacy of touch may succeed where I would fail." He rose from the couch and turned to the girl. "Is your mind still made up, Marta? You will stay, as you planned?"

"I will stay, Kyril," she replied. "As I planned and for the very short while that will be necessary. He will need me when they come, Kyril. Perhaps even the robot will need me. They are two lost souls in the world now, without any friends but you and I, I will be with them at the last moment. I will follow when my presence is no longer needed."

"Where are you going?" called Graeme as Kyril stepped towards an arched entrance.

"Now there," smiled Kyril, "is at last a question that I positively do know that I cannot answer. I have lived seven centuries, Jon. You have lived fifty centuries and I begin to suspect you may live yet for many more. But to all life, material or mental, no matter how prolonged, there will come the End. To you, as to me, and to the Monitors, maybe even to this curious creature of metal who has grown a soul, will come a moment when he will no longer know where he is going, will no longer know what his next step will be . . ."

Fleetly he ran out into the dawn and Graeme ran after him. Marta followed more slowly and Atlas moved his metal bulk ponderously and followed. Kyril poised on the edge of the abyss and flung up both his arms.

"I do not wait for the pains of dissolution," he cried. "I have lived a life of glory in this best of all worlds and I am curious to see what lies beyond . . ."

He leaped and the breezes caught him and fluttered his garment round him. But it could not hold him up and like a plummet he dropped down the awesome chasm, like a stone falling that thousand airy feet. Graeme shuddered and could not look over. Marta came and put an arm round his shoulder and Atlas held one of his arms clumsily. As though they were leading an old, old man, they led him back to the little crystal house.

CHAPTER TWELVE

THE name of Kyril was not mentioned. He had lived and now he had gone. What more could be said of the life of any man? But that there was in the strange girl Marta much of the woman he had known in his youth, was proved by her next words.

"We will go away from here," she said. "This spot will be for ever the place of Kyril. I think he would be content that it shall remain for ever in solitude. We will go to a city."

Graeme was too far sunken in blackness of spirit to answer her and he followed her obediently and Atlas after him, into the flyer. It rose and they hovered over the crystal house. But Marta did not destroy the house; it seemed obvious that it would remain always the monument of the departed Kyril. She had not cried when he had jumped and for a brief instant Graeme wondered dully just what her relationship had been with the man. Had she been wife, sister, or friend? He felt he would never know now nor would he perhaps ever know into what peculiar lines the relationships of the people of Earth had fallen during five millennia. As a man will, while he had been with Marta before, there had strayed through his mind the egregious idea that maybe he and she might mate and bring forth a line of supermen such as he had then thought he was the first. His very soul cringed within him at the thought. Even thought the mere fact of his evil aura precluded that, the thought now seemed somehow sacrilegious. Marta was of a different species to him. She was five millennia further along the evolutionary path. As well expect an angel to couple with an ape.

"Your Monitors," he said suddenly, "they are angels, I think. In my times there were many who believed in such beings. They were supposed to be immortal and immaterial, able to travel with the speed of thought, and they were supposed to surround the throne of the mythical God these people worshipped."

"You *really* were primitive in your Twenty-Third Century, weren't you, Jon?" she laughed as the flyer bore them rapidly southward. "No, the Monitors are not angels. If there are angels no man has ever seen one. But that there is a God, we all know now Jon. It is no longer a matter of believing or disbelieving. The Being who is responsible for the All is vaster and more incomprehensible than any of the many religions Mankind ever dreamed of. But one thing the Monitors share with your 'angels' is that they do in actual fact 'travel' through the Cosmos with the speed of thought."

Graeme tried to digest this but found it quite beyond him. He stared out of the flyer at the land-masses below. "Where are we going?"

"There is a small city in the centre of what was once Australia," she told him. "When I was very young I was one of those who helped to build it. It was in fact one of my educational tasks. It lies in the heart of what was once fierce desert. I think it is small enough to have escaped the notice of the all-conquering Apollo."

The city was indeed intact and they landed outside it and walked in on foot. Night was falling as they approached and the lights in the city were going on automatically. Graeme could still, in his misery, shudder at the thought of all those automatic mechanisms functioning perfectly for centuries, with no human being in the city. For it, like all the others he had seen, was completely empty of life.

They went in to a hall which was furnished richly and in a small corner they sat down, Graeme and Marta with Atlas standing beside them. Graeme had been very fearful of broaching the subject up to now but after the dramatic death of Kyril he felt that now it might not much matter to the girl.

"The radiation death," he began haltingly. "What will it be like? Has it not been known in your world before? After all, the radio-activity within the Earth itself can scarcely have been touched as yet, even after five millennia. Five thousand years is as nothing to the radio-active lives of the heavy elements we knew."

"We had long gone past radio-activity, Jon," she said serenely. "I will admit that these cities were built by the old-time atomic power. But that was when our modern world was in its infancy. Now we build and make by far subtler means. Now we can go straight to the heart of matter and remould it in its very essence so that it assumes the form we wish. That great lesson is one of the great gifts the Monitors brought to us. Our next step is to transcend even that, to obviate mere manipulation and operate upon matter with the powers of the mind itself."

He sat stupefied as she talked. It was not believable. Then he remembered the instantaneous erection of the insubstantial crystal houses he had seen. Built in instants and seeming to be made of light itself, they had been as solid as any granite or marble. His mind felt dulled and weary but he forced himself to listen.

"No, we have had nothing but natural radiation in our world for centuries, Jon," she went on. "The death is peaceful, I learned from Seena and Hans. Of course, even as we are, we have learned some control over our bodily processes and the dissolution of the body can be helped when the commanding intelligence becomes aware that the decay within is too far advanced to avert. Kyril chose a dramatic way to end his life, he had always been curious of the primitive age in which you lived, Jon, in which it seemed men voluntarily suffered pain and anguish and made no attempt to avoid it."

"The world was like that then, Marta," he said bluntly. "It was a world of beauty and cruelty. Its very essence was built upon conflict and struggle. All life preyed upon lower life. It was kill or be killed. And by that very fact man rose from the slime of the beginning, rose through apehood to the semi-divine creature who at last spanned the stars."

She smiled gently. "It is good to see a man loyal to

his age, Jon. That is as it should be. But we have gone on from there, Jon. We have learned many things from ourselves, from studies and meditation and finally from the Monitors."

He moved irritably. "Must I believe in these ... these ... Monitors?"

"Indeed you must, Jon, for they are coming to see you. They are intensely curious to see a man who has lived five millennia and still remains essentially the man he was at birth. Also they are curious I think about the new soul of Atlas. This is a thing they have never encountered before in any galaxy."

Again he cringed inwardly and stared about him with terror. The lights were comforting and also was the massive and silent presence of Atlas, his only link with his old world of the Twenty-Third Century.

"Coming," he mumbled. "You said they travelled with the speed of thought. Why have they not come sooner? Why do they not come at this very instant?"

She laughed musically. "They could span the Cosmos in an instant, Jon, did they wish to. But you must realize that I am only a simple girl. I was born long after they came, stayed and then departed. All that I know of them is what I have learned from the records."

"Legends! Myth!" he said stoutly recovering his spirit a little and she smiled tolerantly. He went on: "We too had many legends of beings who had visited earth, angels, demons, elementals, fairies, imps, a host of imaginary beings, born only in fevered imaginations."

"I will make no attempt to convince you, Jon," she said serenely. "That I can leave safely to more capable minds than mine. I will tell you what I know of them. You can listen or not as you will. The end will be the same when they come."

"When they come!" Terrified he leaped to his feet. "I will take the flyer and go from here. You have led me here for this is the place to which they will come. I will fly ..."

"Sit down, Jon," she smiled. "There is no escape and

when you know at last, what the truth is, you will no longer want to escape."

"Master," came the grating voice of Atlas. "Look, there is Apollo and now it has come to it."

Graeme looked at the screen nearby and saw the starship in a black sky hovering as it seemed in the void. A pencil of light came from the south and licked at the ship. Like a gnat it eluded the light but always the light pursued and as quickly caught it again. Then came a long narrow beam from the north and the two beams joined and at the join was Graeme's great starship. But for an instant only. There came a burst of light that was like the light of a supernova and then the rays winked out and the starship was atoms again.

Graemes' face blanched. "The Monitors have come then? They have reached out and destroyed my ship. They are here already."

"The Monitors did not destroy the ship, Jon. It was our own people who did that. Kyril tried to convince you that the Monitors are in no way our masters. They are our elder brothers. My own people have reached out and obliterated that impious robot and its crew. But as a sanitary measure only, for the entire ship was drenched in your deadly radiation."

"These Monitors," he said feverishly. "What are they like? What forms have they, what sort of bodies? I must know all about them – "

Her laughter trilled through the hall and echoed from the columns.

"Delightful little man," she said. "So you want to know all about our Monitors. So like a primitive man, all curiosity and no prudence, all knowledge and no wisdom. The lower can never know the higher, Jon, it can only grow into brotherhood with the higher. And it is this that the Monitors are leading us along into. As regards form, well, here there is a great difficulty. We on Earth have a form which is preserved all through life, without changing. The Monitors have no one such form. They are able to rearrange the atoms of their organisms to suit whatever environment they choose. They have no absolute "size" and can be giants or protozoa. They can exist in the very core of a star and they can exist in the absolute zero of Space. They know and can control at will all the bodily and mental processes within their organisms and they promise that one day we too will be able to do likewise. Ultimately, they hinted, they will lead us towards a state of being where Matter is finally discarded as the vehicle of Mind, and that our essences will dwell outside of all forms. You see how difficult it all is, Jon. Even Kyril despaired of ever being able to communicate it to you."

"What *species* are they?" asked Graeme in desperation. "If they are not gods or angels, what in heaven's name, are they?"

"In Heaven's name, Jon, as you aptly put it, they are *human beings*."

He dashed a hand across his eyes and laughed crazily. "Now, you go too far. Your semantic barriers have swamped you. I think I should know what a human being is, after five millennia."

"You have never really known what a human being is, Jon," she said tenderly. "My people had never known, until the Monitors came. You have never known until now and very soon, when you will know in truth. I fear that in the beginning very little of it will impinge on your soul. But – they are curious about you, Jon. There is a moment in Time when they will come and look at you and Atlas, Jon, and you will see them. Just what you will see when you look, I cannot tell. In fact, I do not even know whether whatever form they assume will register on your retinas. They are protean, Jon and can be anything they choose. But still, they are *human*. The Monitors are in no way alien to us on this Earth. They are ourselves as we might be and as, with their help, we will one day become."

"Tell me," he said, a new humility coming over him. "This thing is a contradiction in terms and I cannot understand. How can they be human beings if they have such powers, while I who also am human – ?"

"Human they are, Jon," she replied earnestly. "They are human beings in the very highest sense of the word. They are maybe, very close to the top of the ladder of humanity. They are the very flower of humanity. They are very close to being in truth what humanity was first created to be."

He fell silent brooding fearfully, his mind crushed like an ant beneath these great thoughts. His whole being yearned to laugh to scorn these words she was mouthing so serenely, just as though they were true. But somewhere in his total consciousness was now creeping a faint tendril of belief.

"They have found only Earth to bear intelligence at this moment in eternity," she went on absently as though he was not there. "Men in that time thought it strange for such a great company of stars to be the retinue of a ball of mud which by chance bred Mind. But there is a thought here, Jon, which will help. The life of a star, of a galaxy, is so vast and so unthinkably long by our little standards that it is possible that at some other moment in Eternity, in the past or in the future, some other world may breed mind. There is a platform here where our infant minds meet those adult minds of the Monitors. We found that they like us, groped blindly in their conceptions of Eternity and Infinity. They have lived uncounted centuries, each of their entities, and yet they know that compared with Eternity, their long almost immortal lives are but a moment. They have spanned galaxies and the metagalaxy. They have journeyed across the far reaches of Space out beyond the galaxies that are beyond our Galaxy. And always out there are more galaxies and more stars and more universes. And out beyond them there are still more and more stars and still more galaxies. They returned home, Jon, as the weary traveller returns home after a long journey. So, when the mind touches Eternity and Infinity, we and the Monitors are joined by a bond of ignorance and smallness that has been at times in the past, very comforting to some of us. . . ."

Her voice trailed off and Graeme looked at her. She was reclining in a languid posture and her face smiled across at him. "Do not have fear, Jon," she said faintly. "They are truly the summit of Creation. To them you will appear as a precocious infant and Atlas will be a strange new artifact. They will want to study you . . ."

A cold sweat broke out on Graeme's face and he writhed back. She smiled again. "You have the most dreadful primitive imagination, Jon," she said with a tiny laugh. "You imagine they will dissect you to see how your body works. Have no fear of that Jon. I wish that I could wait and see them. But I cannot nor will I. This frame of mine is destroyed now and . . . good-bye, Jon Graeme, and good-bye, Atlas. Maybe Man and Robot, hand in hand, will lead the race a little upwards. . . ."

Her voice trailed away again and this time, Jon Graeme knew it would not sound again. He stared down at her form and his heart almost broke, in loneliness, in desolation, in love. He groped for Atlas and took hold of one of the robot's metal arms. He stared round him in terror. The lights were going out in the great hall. Terrified beyond measure, he clung to the robot and stared at the lights. They were blazing as they had blazed before. How then did it seem they were dimming?

His eyes went up and up and now he saw the reason. A greater light was shining on the city from outside and its radiance had dimmed the light of the material lights within.

Then suddenly, Jon Graeme, born of this Earth five millennia ago, found that he could thrust his fear from him as one discards an unwanted cloak. He stood upright and stretched his body to its full height. With his hand firmly clasped round the metal arm of his friend Atlas the Robot, he raised his face to the roof of the hall.

The light was growing still more in intensity and yet it was a light that did not hurt his eyes. The light seemed to dissolve the very fabric of the rooftops of that city and Jon Graeme and Atlas stood upright still staring upwards as the light grew stronger and stronger and washed round them like a warm and comforting flood.

A TRIPHAMMER THRILLER

The Mobster

By JOHN ROEBURT

FRANK SILCOX –
magnetic, handsome, son of a cop . . . headed for a brilliant career as one of New York's Finest.
FRANKIE SILK –
brutal killer, woman-runner, Bright Young Man in the world of organized crime.
They were as different as night and day – yet they were the same man!
In this penetrating portrait of an embittered, destructive-minded young mobster who rose from fledgling cop to vice lord, John Roeburt has ripped the veil from the age when police and politicians sold out to mobs and hoodlums in an unholy alliance of terror and death.

20p

WORLD DISTRIBUTORS (Manchester) LTD

A TRIPHAMMER THRILLER

The Haunting of Drumroe

By CLAUDETTE NICOLE

Or was she, as they said in the village, a witch like her great-grandmother Monica?
Eileen was afraid. Very afraid. But she had to stay now. She had to find out if she was truly one of the damned . . .

20p

WORLD DISTRIBUTORS (Manchester) LTD

A TRIPHAMMER THRILLER

Shadow Mansion

By WILMA FORREST

Against her will, Madi had been brought to The Mansion.
It had been a prison once. Now it was something else. But nothing could still the silent screams of those who had never left there – alive.
Madi did not fear the evil of the past. There was a new madness that hid in the shadows of the present, a madness she had to seek out and destroy – or else stay locked in that dark world forever.

20p

WORLD DISTRIBUTORS (Manchester) LTD

A TRIPHAMMER THRILLER

Behind the Scarlet Door

By LOU CAMERON

When the case began, Sgt. Morgan Price knew very little about witchcraft. He'd been called in because he spoke Welsh. The murdered girl had come from Wales. And she'd been earning her bread singing Welsh folk songs.

Price knew this case was going to be a weirdo, because the girl had told the police someone had put a curse on her, a curse that would kill her.

And now the men at the lab could not find a mark on her body! Not a clue as to cause of death!

The only thing they did find was that the girl had been dead for nearly two weeks . . . two weeks *before* she herself had come to the police!

20p

WORLD DISTRIBUTORS (Manchester) LTD

A TRIPHAMMER THRILLER

Framed in Guilt

By DAY KEENE

In the competitive world of Hollywood, Robert Stanton had it made. His movies were always profitable, he was engaged to a beautiful actress, he owned a big house, complete with swimming pool. Then the murders began. The first was a girl who claimed to know the secret of his past – and talked about it too much. The second had tried blackmail, but didn't live to collect.

Stanton had an airtight alibi for the first killing. But after the second, the police were openly suspicious. And then came the attempted murder of the boy who was supposed to be his son – a part of his past Stanton claimed not to remember, but somebody else remembered all too well....

20p

WORLD DISTRIBUTORS (Manchester) LTD

A CAMEO ROMANCE

The Truly Lov'd

By VALENTINE

Pretty Lynn Venables is terribly shocked when she returns from her finishing school in France to hear that her childhood boy-friend Larry Martin is serving twelve month under probation in a country job as a motor salesman. But what hurts Lynn more than anything is the fact that Larry has given instructions that nobody – particularly herself – is to be given his address.

The lovely Lynn is also strong-willed and she is determined that, whatever Larry has done, it will not come between them. Here is an interesting situation that Valentine has exploited with his usual skill and charm.

20p

WORLD DISTRIBUTORS (Manchester) LTD

A CAMEO ROMANCE

Log Camp Nurse

By ARLENE J. FITZGERALD

"In spite of her distress, her hands flew to her hair, running quick, automatic fingers through it in an effort to fluff out its soaked, blonde masses. She looked such a mess. But there wasn't time to worry about that. No time at all, for all at once (though she couldn't remember later how it happened) Dr. Russell Bryden was out of the station wagon holding her in his arms. Just for an instant his lips were hard and warm and comforting against her rain-chilled face."

20p

WORLD DISTRIBUTORS (Manchester) LTD

A BANDOLERO WESTERN

Prairie Preacher

By ROD BRANNAN

Down a dark back alley in the town of Marvin Flats a ring of menacing cowboys slowly closed in on Marshal Clint Fairburn determined to show him no mercy.
Sent incognito to find out who was behind the continued gold robberies in the district, Clint had no one to turn to for help and no friends in Marvin Flats.
And yet one man came to his aid, breaking up the fight with his voice alone – Ebenezer Dale, a prairie preacher.
With the preacher's local knowledge and the guns of Sheriff Abe Carson at his disposal, Marshal Fairburn started a relentless search for an unknown opponent – an enemy who knew every move before it was made, a man who would kill ruthlessly and without thought.
And then Kathleen Murray, a girl the Marshal had rescued from a wrecked stagecoach, was kidnapped – and Clint came to realise just how desperate his opponent was . . .

20p

WORLD DISTRIBUTORS (Manchester) LTD

A BANDOLERO WESTERN

Raging Guns

By J. E. GRINSTEAD

Cleek and Tex stayed holed up in the little shack and watched Babe's men shooting at them. They couldn't get out of the shack alive – but no one could get in to kill them, either. And then Babe came up with an idea that was dynamite – two sticks of it. Carefully he lit the fuses and then tossed them at the tiny shack. Cleek watched the two sticks with their spitting fuses as they sailed in the window. There was only one way to get out alive and it meant taking a desperate chance.

But if he had to die, Cleek meant to do it like a man.

20p

WORLD DISTRIBUTORS (Manchester) LTD